The Virtuous Vegan

Gluten-Free, Sugar-Free Cuisine

Dawn Grey, PhD, CHHP

The Virtuous Vegan
Gluten-Free, Sugar-Free Cuisine
Dawn Grey, PhD, CHHP

Visit our website at www.newdawnkitchen.com

Library of Congress Cataloging-in-Publication Data

ISBN-10: 1452896534
ISBN-13: 9781452896533

Printed in the United States of America

Acknowledgements

This is my second cookbook, and would not be possible without the encouragement of my readers of "New Dawn Kitchen: Gluten-Free, Vegan, and Easily Sugar-Free Desserts", my clients, Facebook fans, and those of you who took the time to personally email me and thank me for sharing my recipes. There are a few others who deserve special mention, as without them, this book would not have been written:

The Daiya Cheese Company, for making the yummiest gluten-free, vegan cheeses on the planet. Before your products, my Italian food tasted like plastic, and my Mexican food like rubber. Without realizing it, you have provided full liberation to those who cannot eat traditional cheese, making cooking and eating joyful again, and have enabled me to fool even the most critical taste buds. Thank you for featuring my Macaroni and Cheese recipe on your website.

To the makers of Mimic Crème, a heartfelt thank you for enabling me to make Alfredo, creamy soups, and the best coffee drinks I have had since I had to forfeit dairy. My life is richer because of you ☺ (get it? Ha!)

My husband, Mark, who once again endured the kitchen messes and my talking out loud phases. This time, no exploding cakes, and you have to admit my gluten-free macaroni and cheese is flawless.

Finally, to my feline friend, Twilight, aka Yogi Purrananda. We did it again. I know there are other books and cookbooks yet to come of our collaborative efforts, and completing this project is simply the beginning of the next one. One of these days, I am going to write a book about you. Om. Purr. Om.

Table of Contents

To The Reader

The recipes contained within these pages are the result of many years of modifying and taste testing, by myself and those who would never consciously eat gluten-free or vegan. Most of the time, they had no idea they were eating, other than it was really good food.

It is not my goal to try to educate the public as to why they should eat gluten-free, vegan, or watch their sugar and sodium intake. While there is much I could say on these subject matters, this is a celebration of food and not a health guide. There is much that can be said about our need to eliminate chemicals and fast food from our diet, but that is not for me to say here. Instead, I chose to focus my attention on what you can have. To those that are gluten-free and/or vegan, I am here to provide you with options and not with excerpts of research and case studies. You bought this book because you or the recipient needs to eat this way.

It is my belief that while food is fuel, it is meant to be enjoyed and celebrated. There is no reason to ever eat something you do not like, nor do I believe you should ever eat food that taste less than delicious. For those, like me, who are suddenly presented with an immediate reason to give up an entire food group, this can create quite a challenge.

These pages contain 144 recipes that I simply adore, and I believe you will, too. Of the many hundreds that I have from my own kitchen, In addition to taste, I chose to feature these 144 because of their ease of preparation, availability of ingredients, and affordability. Buying already made gluten-free and/or vegan meals can be expensive; making your own, with their special flours and ingredients can be costly, too. The convenience of simple foods prepared deliciously is what I am all about. There is no need to make something different for the one whose diet needs special consideration. Everyone can share the same foods with equal enjoyment.

Namaste,

Dawn Grey

Introduction

We have all experienced moments in our lives when we realize our lives have changed forever. These moments forever define our character. I believe it is not what happens to us but how we react to what happens to us that ultimately shapes our life experience. While I have had my ups and downs in life like anyone else, from dealing with a family member's chronic illness to my own struggles with weight, nothing has impacted my life more than the realization that there are some foods that I cannot eat without severe impact to my health and well-being: dairy, egg yolks, shellfish, and wheat and gluten containing foods (primarily limited to the cooler months of the year). While the omission of shellfish was no big deal, as I have been a vegetarian more on than off since age 17, the impact of losing wheat, gluten, and dairy were immense. I love vegetables and primarily eat vegan anyways, but wheat? What was I to do about bread? Pasta? What about baking?

I am the go to girl in my group when it comes to baking. I am not a baker by training or profession. However I have the knack in duplicating a dessert recipe if I take the time to eat it slowly, examine its texture, and carefully pay attention to its scent, color, and weight. I will even admit that I can create a recipe that often I myself cannot bake with initial success (hence the thank you to my husband and comment about exploding cakes) until I play with it a few times. But ultimately, I am the one who makes yummy treats, supports bake sales for schools and churches, and the one that everyone hopes will get her ovens going for Christmas. I normally eat healthy, so my consumption of cookies is limited to tastes of the finished product, so removing them initially was not a problem. And then one day that avoidance came crashing down around me. It was my birthday, and my husband went all out to create a surprise celebration for me and several of my friends. A limo ride to my favorite restaurant in Kansas City. An entire portion of the restaurant was reserved just for us. The finale was a gorgeous cake, my birthday cake, being hoisted by a proud waiter. It was a beautiful, heavily frosted, work of art. I knew that I wanted it. I also knew that I had not informed my husband of my suspicions of having wheat/gluten intolerance. Everyone else was digging into my cake and loving it. So to not hurt feelings, to "fit in" and most important, to feel "normal", I took a small slice I had a couple of bites, and it really was wonderful. I figured I had enough to taste but not enough to create discomfort. I was unfortunately not that lucky.

For those of you who suffer from Celiac disease, lactose intolerance, or any other food that falls under the category of intolerance or sensitivity (allergies can be serious but often affect people differently than an intolerance) you are all too familiar with stomach pain so bad you feel you have been poisoned, spasms in the GI tract that have you convinced an alien being is about to break out of your body and rip you in half, and/or intestinal issues so severe you promise yourself you will never eat anything ever again, you know what my next 16 hours of life were like. It was a day I would never want to redo again. Not only was I feeling horrible, on my birthday with this great party in progress, but I never wanted to have to feel that I had to avoid enjoying some of life's culinary pleasures because of my fussy tummy. I had enough of that my entire childhood, and I was not about to spend my adult life as a "baby who never outgrew colic" as my mother put it. At the very least, I wanted to be able to have a slice of cake on my birthday, apple pie on Thanksgiving, and a Christmas cookie. Most of the time, I eat so healthy I scare people. My love of green vegetables and my declaration of being a "vegeholic" on Facebook and other blogs are what I am known for these days. However, there are days when I want to end my yummy cabbage in sauce dinner with a cookie or two with some almond milk. Store bought ones are a gamble. Some are good, others are so bad I think the packaging would be more tasty. But no store bought item, regardless of how good it is, can substitute for the experience that only your own baking can bring. There is something to the smell of warm cinnamon rolls rising in the oven, its aroma wafting through the kitchen that cannot be replaced by eating a bowl of gluten-free vegan oatmeal with a sprinkle of cinnamon and maple syrup.

I ran into similar issues when it came to pasta. As an Italian who became vegetarian at age 17 because I simply felt better not eating meat, many of my dinners were pasta based. In my pre-dairy allergy days, some combination of wheat and cheese was in just about every meal I ate. Perhaps it was that over-consumption of wheat and dairy that triggered things, but I could no longer eat the way I wanted to, and I also knew that after all this time I did not want to return to my meat eating days, as that felt wrong in my body as well. I could reduce my sweets. While yummy, no one really needs to eat cookies, regardless of what their ingredients are. But I needed real food to eat every day, and I was not ready to subsist on fruit and nuts. I wanted hot fresh foods that I could eat and feed to other people.

As a certified holistic health practitioner with a PhD in my field, I have immense training in dietary wellness, nutrition, how allergies and intolerances can diminish health, and numerous methods including fasting, detoxification, supplementation, and herbal recipes galore to assist in achieving wholeness and recovery. What my 10+ years of training failed to share with me was one single recipe for those who suffer from any of these conditions. The only official remedy I could suggest to my clients was abstinence. Just as diets do not work because of the limits and deprivation they usually employ, health via abstinence is not always easy, even for those who get immensely sick from a bite of a brownie. What was needed was not only awareness of these conditions, but also a viable option so they did not feel they were missing out. It was at that moment, while friends were gleefully celebrating my birthday, when my work took a whole new turn. My mission would be to create treats that were just as good, if not better, than the goodies I had been known for. While I did not realize it then, it was on that day, October 4, 2001 that the New Dawn Kitchen officially began.

In time, I devised recipes that I shared with local clients during holistic coaching sessions. (My practice is primarily focused on assisting those identify hidden causes of excess weight and decreased energy.) Not only were they enjoying the snack samples, but they wanted the recipes themselves. They also wanted more than just cake, such as pasta and their comfort foods back, so back to the kitchen I went. When my clients were no longer sabotaging their gluten/wheat-free diets, they began to really feel and look better. Their children and partners ate meals with them, most without ever suspecting a thing. At the encouragement of friends and clients, I share this book with all of you who need to follow a restricted diet. Yes, you can have your cake and eat it too, and bread and pancakes and donuts and waffles and all sorts of otherwise off-limits foods.

What is Gluten?

Gluten is the protein that naturally occurs in the following grains: wheat, rye, barley, durum, semolina, einkorn, graham, bulgur, couscous, spelt, farro, kamut, and triticale. Commercial oats also contain gluten due to cross contamination in processing, but actually are gluten-free otherwise. Depending on your level of sensitivity will depend if you can use regular oats or if you need to invest in oats that specifically indicate they are gluten-free. I myself am not sensitive enough for the cross-contamination of oats, so I buy regular oats, which are more affordable and certainly easier to obtain. I would consult with your healthcare provider or nutritionist as to whether or not you can handle oats, or any product for that matter, that is processed on equipment or manufactured in the same environment, as a gluten product.

Therefore, gluten will be present in these grains flours and byproducts, such as barley malt, beer, and many flavorings and spices. When in doubt, obtain vanilla, spices, and any food product that says gluten-free, as gluten is in many products you may not expect it to be, for example, cooking spices. Read everything.

What Grains and Flours are Gluten-Free?

Corn flour, cornmeal, and cornstarch
Buckwheat and buckwheat flour
Rice flour- white and brown
Quinoa, quinoa cereal flakes, and quinoa flour
Millet and millet flour
Sorghum flour
Amaranth and amaranth flour
Certified gluten-free oats and oatmeal
Coconut flour
Teff flour
Nut meals and flours- almond, chestnut, pecan, cashew
Garbanzo, fava bean, pea, soy and other bean flours
Tapioca pearls and tapioca starch/flour (they are the same product)
Potato starch
Potato flour (which is different than potato starch)
Sweet potato and yam flour
Arrowroot starch

Why Eat Wheat/Gluten-Free?

There is a growing awareness that a number of individuals experience mild to severe gastro-intestinal distress when eating wheat/gluten containing foods. While most individuals are more likely to have sensitivity to these foods if eaten in excess, there are those who have allergies to wheat or gluten and therefore cannot safely eat even a small portion of the culprit food.

Another concern is Celiac Disease, a condition in which a person is intolerant to gluten containing foods. In the body of someone with this condition, consuming gluten containing food sets off an autoimmune response that causes damage to the small intestine. This, in turn, causes the small intestine to lose the ability to absorb nutrients, leading to malnutrition, permanent intestinal damage, and possibility of requiring surgery.

There is a belief that removing gluten as well as casein, a protein found in dairy, helps children with Autism Spectrum Disorder. Some parents report improvements in autism symptoms with this dietary regimen. Little actual research has been done, however, on the gluten-free/casein-free diet for autism. However, since there is no dietary need for gluten or casein in the diet, so there is no harm in removing them if they help you or your child's health.

For those who find that eating wheat and/or gluten containing foods creates mild to moderate distress, it is recommended to follow an elimination diet and consult with a healthcare provider and/or dietician for further assistance. In my situation, my gluten intolerance is seasonal, spanning the winter months, whereas my egg yolk and dairy allergies are constant. If you approach your body with awareness, you will know what to do.

Dairy Products: To Eat Or Not To Eat

While most of us are familiar with lactose intolerance and milk allergies, there are other reasons why more and more individuals are reducing or eliminating dairy from their diets. In this age of environmental awareness, using plant-based milk substitutes is more popular due to their smaller impact on environmental waste. Also, for those who are concerned about animal cruelty, avoiding milk helps reduce factory farming practices. Since most dairy cows are supplied with antibiotics, hormones, and fed food that is laced with pesticides, it may be best if we all took a step away from dairy.

For those of you who are vegan (choose to eliminate all animal products), dairy allergic, or lactose intolerant, follow the recipes using whatever milk substitute you wish. You will also find that many of the recipes call for yogurt, cheese, and/or sour cream. For convenience I will call these "milk product", "vegan sour cream", and "non-dairy yogurt " and "vegan cheddar" the first time, and from there, just yogurt, milk, etc. If you bought this book because of your gluten/wheat sensitivity and are not following a dairy-free guideline, feel free to use whatever dairy products you wish in equal measure.

I want to take a moment to discuss the flavor of non-dairy products. If you are very new to dairy alternatives, please note that not all dairy-free milks, cheeses, and other products taste the same. While most would say that they could not tell the difference between one brand of 2% milk from another, I assure you there is major variety in texture, flavor, sweetness, etc between rice and soy milk, and even among the individual brands of soy milk. Be patient, try many brands, and stick with what you love. For me, I really had a hard time with the vegan cheeses, as casein, a common ingredient in dairy-free cheeses, is actually a milk protein, and hence, not dairy-free. The first time I discovered this, I shot out a nasty email to a company, claiming they were falsely advertising their soy cheese, and that if I had wanted dairy, I would have saved $3 and bought real cheese. They apologized, and a week later, a drop shipment of numerous bags of their assorted shredded cheeses were on my doorstep. At first I was really angry, as I made it clear that I am so sensitive to dairy that I get high fevers (105°F) and often need hospitalization if I had more than an accidental taste. I had just recovered from such an episode that luckily I was able to heal from at home, and I felt this really showed their inability to understand that dairy means anything that comes from milk from an animal. Lactose and casein and whey are all different dairy by-products and you can be highly allergic to casein and not be lactose intolerant.

So I stayed away from all cheese, even the truly vegan ones because those that did not have casein tasted like slippery plastic. And then one day I found Daiya cheese online, and my ability to cook and eat my favorite mac and cheese, lasagna, and everything else was restored. Even my husband will eat Daiya cheese. I made a pot of my macaroni and cheese for the 4th of July and those that ate it did not know. I actually took it to be a major compliment when my sister-in-law said it "tasted like Velveeta" because until now, there was no vegan cheese that could fool the taste buds.

I must stress that I am not affiliated with any of the brands I should mention in these pages, but in some cases, like Daiya and Mimic Crème, there was no other alternative (in my opinion) that even came close, and until their emergence, that chapter of my cooking experience was closed. Now, it's re-opened. This book would not exist without those few companies who went out of their way to cater to those of us who cannot or will not consume the traditional products.

Fats: The Good, The Bad, And The Ugly

Remember when margarine first came out and we thought it was healthful to smear gobs of it on our food to get the healthful polyunsaturated fats? Well, like most other food trends, the good and the bad fats list keeps getting updated. Here is my take on fats, as far as this cookbook is concerned: use what is readily available to you. While I am the first to say NO to traditional shortening and lard, if you prefer these, then use them. True they are bad for you, but let's be honest- unless you have an extreme food problem, even the most rich and decadent meal eaten in moderation and not on a daily basis should be fine for your health and your waistline. However, I am the first to say that I love good food, and overindulged a few too many times in the writing of this book.

The main fat most of us need to substitute in dairy-free and vegan cooking is butter. Butter in many ways may actually be healthier than the trans fats in most margarines, but for those who cannot or will not have dairy, both products are likely unsafe to use. My suggestion for recipes that really need a "stick" of butter is to use vegan brands such as "Earth Balance". The buttery blend one is quite tasty on gluten-free toast, but again, fat is fat, so a little goes a long way.

The newest "fat" to get attention these days is coconut oil. Coconut oil is reported to have antibiotic and even weight loss benefits when used moderately. Use common sense. Tablespoons of fat of any kind is not a weight loss tonic, but having the right essential fats in the right quantities is healthful. Some brands are pricier than others, but I have learned that the higher the price, usually the better the buttery flavor. The lower priced ones in general smell and taste like coconut, so keep this in mind. Some cookie recipes taste wonderful with this coconut flavor, whereas other recipes it is just too overpowering, so a higher grade of coconut oil is needed. However, even the lower cost coconut oil can be more than seven dollars for a jar that is smaller than a jar of spaghetti sauce and you might wind up using the whole thing, if not more, for one recipe.

Therefore when I bake cakes and prepare recipes that require a lot of oil, I rely on either canola or extra light olive oil. If you prefer another oil besides olive or canola oil, simply substitute that oil for the butter or oil called for in a recipe. I especially like coconut oil is Asian recipes.

Need To Reduce Fat?

While our recipes will be naturally cholesterol-free because we have omitted all animal products, almost all of our recipes contain oil, margarine, cheese, or all. However, most are not considered low-fat. For those of you who need or want to reduce the fat, there are a number of substitutions you can use.

One of the most popular is to use less oil and more water to sauté in. For baking, applesauce works well in baking recipes, as does pumpkin, mashed sweet potato, or any gluten-free pureed fruit or baby food. If you are already using one of these for your egg replacement, be careful not to add too much, or your recipe will be too wet. My overall suggestion is to use less cooking oil, less oil in dressings, and more broth, vinegar, water, or non-fat liquids whenever possible. You can also go lighter on the cheese, sour cream, etc. I would prefer to just eat a smaller portion of something cheesy and higher in fat, like lasagna, and then fill up on a low fat salad or soup as more of the main dish on those days.

Egg-Free Cooking

If you are vegan or cannot consume eggs or egg yolks like me, you have several options to use as substitutes. Unlike swapping oils and milk for another product, not every egg substitute will work for every recipe, so removing eggs from a recipe is perhaps just as tricky, if not more so, than making the gluten-free switch. My experience is that if you have a recipe that uses 3 or more eggs, you will find it harder to have successful results with an egg substitute. However, it can be done if you take the time to experiment with which product mimics the best texture for your recipe. Most of my recipes will use a product called Ener-G Egg Replacer, which I refer to as egg replacer. In baking, which this cookbook does not really explore (see my other book The New Dawn Kitchen: Gluten-Free, Vegan, and Easily Sugar-Free Desserts) you will see other options, such as tofu or flaxseed meal with water. Do your research and use what you are most comfortable using for your egg replacement. Those who eat eggs can use real eggs/egg whites for the number of egg replacer portions I mention.

Want To Reduce Sugar?

In standard recipes, agave nectar nectar, maple syrup, or any liquid sweetener that is gluten-free will work fine. Barley Malt is not gluten-free, but often sits on store shelves immediately next to rice syrup, which is. When substituting a liquid sweetener for granulated in your own recipes, reduce liquid in recipe by ¼ cup. I am very sugar sensitive, so for my own baking, I use artificial sweetener and/or sugar-free maple syrup, then use 1/3 of the sugar called for in the recipe. While artificial sweeteners are not healthful in the least, this is one of those choices I need to make. I use stevia for granulated sweetening and sugar-free maple syrup mixed with a bit of rice syrup for my liquid sweetening. While maple syrup, rice syrup and agave nectar nectar are more healthful choices, they still have a sugar content that spike my blood sugar if I have more than a couple of bites. I actually prefer rice syrup and use it sparingly as a caramel sauce substitute on rice cream.

Honey is an animal product and is not in theory truly vegan, but locally gathered honey has loads of health benefits, especially for allergy sufferers. I often take a spoonful of honey all winter long to help offset my seasonal allergies. It's just a spoonful, but I find it's like a natural vaccine for me. I also realize this makes me less-than vegan, and I call myself "vegan-enough". Make conscious choices with what you put in your body, as you are the one who has to answer for your health and well-being.

Ultimately the choice is yours when it comes to sweetening your goods. Remember when using a liquid sweetener, use less than the amount of sugar called for unless my recipe already calls for a liquid sweetener (taste test to adjust sweetness level). Adjust the liquid by two tablespoons less to begin with.

Substitutes For Cream And Condensed Milk Products

Recently I discovered a groovy product named Mimic Crème that works for those of us who need a gluten-free vegan cream product. It is on the grocery shelf in one of those aseptic containers that soymilk comes in, but refrigerate after opening. I make the most awesome Italian food such as Alfredo with this, but you can use plain soy or rice milk instead. It's not much higher in fat than either option, but may be harder to locate. I would say Mimic Crème goes into that same category as Daiya cheese- offering gluten-free vegan freedom for those of us who must abstain from the traditional, and as such, all sorts of recipes, such as a good cup of coffee, is back in my life.

Peanut Free/Nut Free

For a nut-free peanut butter substitute try using sunflower seed butter, commonly found as the product "Sunbutter" in recipes. Sesame seed butter (also called tahini) is another choice, but requires (in my opinion) a touch of liquid sweetener to offset its savory taste. Other seed and nut butters include macadamia nut butter, cashew butter, pecan butter, and my favorite, almond butter. You may want to sweetener or salt the recipe differently depending on your like for salt and sweet. You can also use soynuts in recipes or for snacks in equal measure as you would use other nuts. I don't use too many nuts in my cooking, as my body cannot handle too much fat in any quantity, so I reserve my nut portions for the occasional peanut butter sandwich craving, or a handful of cashews with some raisins as a quick snack.

Salt-Free

There are a number of potassium salt products out there for those who must watch their sodium intake. All are fine, but please do not use an herbal blend like Mrs. Dash for baking! Feel free to use in equal measure or less, as potassium salt, as far as I am concerned, seems more salty and concentrated.

Breakfasts

They say breakfast is the most important meal of the day, but when you live a gluten-free vegan lifestyle, often oatmeal (if you can tolerate gluten-free oats) and fruit are the main events on the menu.

If you like big breakfasts and brunches, call your friends. Waffles, bagels, pancakes, crepes, and even donuts are on the menu again. Enjoy!

Bagels

Growing up immediately outside of NYC, there were bagel shops everywhere. They were these big rounds of bread with all sorts of toppings and flavors from blueberry to sesame to "everything". They are a lot of work, but they freeze well, so I suggest doubling or even tripling the recipe.

3 cups gluten-free all-purpose flour
1 teaspoon salt
2 teaspoons flax meal
1½ teaspoons egg replacer
1 tablespoon xanthan gum
1 tablespoon yeast
2 tablespoons agave nectar nectar
2 tablespoons vegetable oil
1 teaspoon cider vinegar
1¼ cups warm water
1 teaspoon granulated sweetener
extra flour, for dusting rolling surface
cornmeal, for dusting pan

Line a baking pan or cookie sheet with parchment paper and sprinkle it with cornmeal. Put some flour on a second baking pan or cookie sheet. Put Flour, salt, flax meal, egg replacer, xanthan gum, and yeast into a mixing bowl and whisk together.

In a separate bowl, whisk together agave nectar, oil, vinegar, and 1¼ cups warm water. Using a mixer, slowly incorporate the liquid mixture into dry ingredients. Add more warm water, if necessary, to create smooth consistency. Mixture may be quite thick. Beat on medium-high speed for 3 minutes.

Lightly roll dough in the flour and roll into a ball. Flatten the ball slightly and poke a hole in the center. Repeat until all the dough is used. Place each bagel on the baking pan sprinkled with cornmeal. Allow bagels to rise, about 20 to 30 minutes. Once bagels have risen, bring a skillet of water to boil. Preheat oven to 375°F. Drop a few bagels into the boiling water. Simmer for 30 seconds, turn over and cook for another 30 seconds. Using a slotted spoon, remove bagels, drain, and put bagels back on same baking pan. Once all bagels are boiled, bake them for 25 minutes. Cool on a rack.

Stuffed French Toast

This works well for a brunch or breakfast gathering. I brought this to my church one Sunday, and it disappeared quite quickly. Nobody knew what they were, or in this case, were not eating.

2 cups mixed berries, fresh or frozen
½ teaspoon lemon juice
½ teaspoon lemon zest
5 tablespoons granulated sweetener, divided
8 slices gluten-free bread, cut into ½-inch cubes
1 cup milk product (I prefer vanilla flavored almond for this recipe)
2 teaspoons vanilla extract
¼ teaspoon baking powder
Egg replacer for 4 eggs, prepared according to box instructions
2 teaspoons coconut oil

Preheat oven to 400°F. Grease a 9inch pie dish or a 9x9 inch baking pan. Mix together berries, lemon juice, lemon zest and 2 tablespoons sugar. Set aside. Place half the bread cubes in the bottom of prepared dish. Place fruit evenly over the bread. Spread remaining bread cubes over the fruit, covering as much as possible.

Mix remaining ingredients together in a mixing bowl until well blended. Pour liquid mixture over the bread and fruit. Make sure all the bread is coated with liquid. Place dish in oven and cook for 20 to 30 minutes until bread begins to brown and most of the liquid has been absorbed. Allow to cool for a few minutes before serving.

Waffles

I had put away my waffle iron before I created this recipe. Most of the gluten-free mixes contained dairy, and the ones that did not made waffles as heavy as lead and as doughy as a sponge. Feel free to experiment with other flavors and extracts. Just make sure everything is gluten-free and you'll be fine.

Egg replacer for 4 eggs, prepared according to box instructions
5 tablespoons granulated sweetener
¼ cup vegan butter or vegetable oil
1 cup milk product
1 teaspoon vanilla
2 cups white rice flour
2 teaspoons xanthan gum
1 tablespoon baking powder
1 teaspoon salt
½ ripe mashed banana
1 tablespoon almond or other nut butter

Prepare egg replacer according to instructions and add sweetener. Stir together in a large bowl until well-combined. Add oil, milk, banana, almond butter and vanilla, and stir gently.

In a separate bowl, mix together flour, xanthan gum, baking powder and salt. Add to egg mixture and beat on low speed until well combined. Batter should be thick.

Pour a small portion of batter into a well-oiled waffle iron and cook until done. Repeat until all batter is used. Top with additional sliced bananas, nuts, and syrup or agave nectar nectar.

Breakfast Crepés

Technically, you can serve these any time of the day. I pack mine with tons of fruit, but for lunch or dinner, try mushrooms and cheese and omit the vanilla and sweetener.

1 cup brown rice flour
3 tablespoons granulated sweetener
1 cup milk product
Egg replacer for 2 eggs, prepared according to box instructions
1 teaspoon vanilla
1 teaspoon oil
Your choice of fresh or canned fruit, such as blueberry pie filling
vegan whipped cream, syrup, or other toppings, optional

Mix flour and sugar in a blender or mixing bowl. Prepare egg replacer according to instructions, and add milk and vanilla and combine well. Batter should be thin, like cake batter. If it's too runny, add more flour, a tablespoon at a time.

Place oil in a heavy skillet or non-stick pan and heat skillet to medium high. Pour only enough batter into the skillet to coat the bottom of the pan, not enough to make pancakes. Tilt the pan until batter is evenly distributed. Cook until bubbles cover the crepé. Gently lift one corner to check the bottom. Cook until bottom is lightly browned. Repeat until all batter is used.

Fill with your choice of fruit or filling and top as desired.

Pancakes

I went through a lot of batters before deciding on this one. Most gluten-free pancake batters yielded pancakes that were really heavy and thick no matter how much liquid I used, but this one is just right. Chances are, no one will know the difference.

1 cup brown rice flour
½ cup sorghum flour
½ cup garbanzo flour
2 tablespoons baking powder
¼ teaspoon salt
¼ teaspoon ground cinnamon
1¼ cups unflavored club soda or seltzer water, room temperature, divided
Egg replacer for 3 eggs, mixed with seltzer instead of water
1 tablespoon of oil
2 tablespoons agave nectar or maple syrup
4 tablespoons oil, vegan butter, or non-stick spray for cooking

In a large bowl, sift or whisk all the dry ingredients. In a separate bowl, whisk half the soda water with the egg replacer, agave nectar/syrup until blended. Add mixture to the flour mixture and stir until just combined. Batter may have small lumps.

Add remaining soda water and gently stir. Do not over mix. Heat a non-stick griddle or large skillet and coat with non-stick spray, butter, or oil. Pour 2 to 3 tablespoons of batter onto the pan and cook until the surface is covered with small bubbles that begin to pop, about 1½ to 2 minutes. Flip pancakes and cook the other side for another minute or until golden brown.

Cinnamon Raisin Biscuits

Buckwheat and garbanzo flours add protein and nutrients, making this recipe more suitable for breakfast. It is one of those recipes that is great to bring to a gathering to show them how a gluten-free vegan lifestyle is not one of deprivation.

¾ cup garbanzo flour
½ cup brown rice flour
½ cup buckwheat flour
¼ cup tapioca starch
2 teaspoons baking powder
½ teaspoon sea salt
1 teaspoon cinnamon
½ teaspoon xanthan gum
¾ cup vegan butter, coconut oil or vegetable shortening
1 tablespoon agave nectar nectar
¾ cup milk product
½ cup raisins
biscuit glaze, see below
½ cup rice syrup or other liquid sweetener
1 tablespoon Mimic crème or milk substitute

Preheat oven to 400°F. Line a cookie sheet with parchment paper. In a medium bowl, combine first 8 ingredients. Using a fork or pastry blender, cut butter into dry ingredients until mixture is crumbly.

Pour in agave nectar and milk and stir. Fold in raisins. Scoop batter out with a large spoon and place 12 even sized scoops on sheet. Bake for 15 minutes or until toothpick comes out clean, rotating pans about halfway through.

To make the glaze, combine rice syrup and milk in a small bowl. Drizzle icing over biscuit tops while biscuits are still warm.

Granola

This is an all-purpose recipe that is equally good as a cereal, topping for non-dairy ice cream, or as the basis of granola bars.

1 cup gluten-free oats

½ cup chopped walnuts

¼ cup toasted pumpkin seeds

¼ cup maple syrup

1 tablespoon rice syrup

1 teaspoon cinnamon

¼ cup raisins

1 teaspoon vanilla extract

Combine oats, walnuts, pumpkin seeds, and coconut in a greased 13x 9 baking pan and set aside. In a saucepan over medium heat, combine syrups and cinnamon; bring to a boil. Cook and stir for 1 minute. Remove from the heat; stir in vanilla and raisins. Pour over oat mixture and toss to coat. Bake at 275° F for 30-40 minutes or until golden brown, stirring every 10 minutes. Cool, stirring occasionally. Store in an airtight container. Stays fresh for about 1 week.

Congee

Congee is an Asian rice porridge commonly served at breakfast, often with eggs. My good friend Ashley first introduced me to this, and I have been playing around with the recipe ever since. I suggest using pan fried tofu to provide protein. Experiment with Congee. You can use vegetable broth instead of water for a flavorful rice dish for lunch or dinner.

1 cup short-grain rice

up to 8 cups water

Salt to taste

½ cup roasted peanuts, chopped, optional

Wash rice and put it in a large pot with 4 cups of water. Bring to a boil, and reduce heat to low. Simmer for about 1 ½ hours, stirring occasionally and adding water as necessary, about 2 to 4 cups more. Salt to taste. Serve hot in individual bowls and garnish with peanuts or pan fried tofu, if desired.

Doughnuts

I know, there is nothing healthy about doughnuts for breakfast, but recipe becomes more "virtuous" because they are baked. Also, this recipe uses the mini doughnut pan, made by Norpro, so if you are good, you will not overdo it. I love these with chocolate soymilk or an iced coffee drink.

1 cup Gluten- Free All-Purpose Flour
¼ cup cocoa powder
½ cup granulated sweetener
2 teaspoons baking powder
¼ teaspoon salt
½ cup milk product (I use chocolate flavored)
1 teaspoon vanilla extract
1 egg replacer portion for one egg, prepared according to box instructions
4 tablespoons vegan butter or coconut oil

Preheat oven to 350° F. Grease donut pan. In a large bowl, combine dry ingredients and mix thoroughly. Combine wet ingredients in a small sauce pan over medium low heat and mix until the butter/coconut oil is melted. Add wet to dry and mix until just combined.

Spoon batter into pan until 2/3 of the way full to allow for rising during the baking process. Bake for 6 minutes, rotate pan, and bake another 6 minutes or until a toothpick comes out clean. Allow to cool completely before removing from pan and adding optional decorations.

Scrambled Tofu with Cheese Grits

On those days when I am really hungry and miss a traditional breakfast, I make this. The cooked grits store well for leftovers.

Grits Ingredients

¾ cup dry grits
3 cups water
1 cup shredded vegan cheddar cheese
Egg replacer for one egg, prepared according to package instructions
2 tablespoons of vegan butter
pinch of salt or salt substitute

Preheat oven to 350°F. Bring water to boil and stir in grits and cook according to package directions. After cooked, pour into a 1-½ quart casserole dish. Mix in the butter, prepared egg replacer and cheese, stirring constantly until thoroughly mixed. Bake uncovered for 30 minutes or until top is set and lightly puffy. Let stand 5 minutes before serving.

Scrambled Tofu

1 tablespoon olive oil
2 green onions, chopped, both green and white parts
1 (14.5 ounce) can peeled and diced tomatoes, drained
1 (12 ounce) package firm tofu, drained and mashed
1 teaspoon of nutritional yeast
salt and pepper to taste
pinch of turmeric

Heat olive oil in a medium skillet over medium heat, and sauté green onions until tender. Stir in tomatoes and mashed tofu. Season with salt, pepper, turmeric, and nutritional yeast. Reduce heat, and simmer until heated through.

Corncakes

These little rounds remind me of what country restaurants serve in little baskets lined with red checkered paper.

1 cup of fine gluten-free corn meal
2/3 cup of rice flour
4 ½ teaspoons of baking powder
2 teaspoons of granulated sweetener
½ teaspoon of salt
Egg replacer for 2 eggs, prepared according to package instructions
1 ¼ cups of unsweetened milk product
2 tablespoons of melted vegan butter or coconut oil
oil for brushing the pan

Stir together the dry ingredients in a bowl. Whisk the egg replacer and milk together in a large bowl. Gradually beat in the dry ingredients and, when well combined, stir in the melted margarine.

Heat two oiled griddle or non-stick frying pans (skillets) and use a tablespoon to drop the batter onto the very hot surface. Make the pancakes about 2 inches in diameter. Once the base is cooked and golden brown, turn the pancake over and cook the other side until they are cooked through.

Serve the cakes straight from the griddle on heated plates with maple syrup or agave nectar nectar and your choice of vegan butter or coconut oil if desired.

Blueberry Banana Oat Muffins

Most people may not know this, but oats are actually gluten-free. They are easily contaminated on machinery as well as being grown too close to a gluten-based grain, however, so if you are highly sensitive to gluten, opt for gluten-free oats. They are pricier, but chances are, they are safe for you. When in doubt, ask your healthcare provider or nutritionist if oats are safe for you. If not, use quinoa flakes.

4 bananas
½ cup oil
½ cup maple syrup or other liquid sweetener
1 cup brown rice flour
1 ½ cups gluten free oats
1 teaspoon cinnamon
½ cup fresh blueberries
1 teaspoon salt
3 teaspoon baking powder
1 tablespoon ground flax seed meal

Preheat oven to 350°F. Grease muffin tin or use liners. Mash the bananas with the maple syrup and oil. Add dry ingredients and mix well. Gently fold in blueberries, being careful not to break them. Spoon batter into muffin pan. Bake 15 minutes, rotate pan, and continue to bake another 10 minutes or until a toothpick comes out clean.

Fruit

I spent almost an entire summer indulging on almost exclusively fruit simply because it was too hot to cook! As such I accumulated tons of recipes, and these are my favorite 12 fruit recipes. With a small amount of nuts or vegan yogurt, you would be surprised how versatile and filling fruit meals can be.

Upside Down Pineapples

When I realized I could not eat the cake, I ate the topping! Now, even though I have created a safe Upside Down Cake (page 56 of New Dawn Kitchen) I still make just the pineapples. It's certainly easier and better for me, and I just love it.

1 pineapple, cut into rings, or 1 can of rings, including juice

1 teaspoon of cinnamon

¼ cup vegan butter, melted

½ cup any liquid sweetener

Preheat oven to 350°F. Spray a 9x13 cake pan with non-stick spray.

Place half of the melted butter in the bottom of the pan, and tilt it to help spread.

Place rings in the cake pan, one at a time. Do not layer pineapple.

Drizzle the rest of the melted butter over the rings along with the liquid sweetener. Sprinkle cinnamon on top.

Bake, uncovered, for 30 minutes, or until golden and bubbly. I like to serve these warm, with a sprinkle of nuts and granola in the morning, or with a small amount of vegan ice cream for a dessert.

Dawn's Very Fruity Salad

Certainly, you can use any fruit you want that is in season, but this is my favorite combination. Go crazy and top it with vegan whipped cream.

2 cups pineapple chunks

2 medium ripe bananas, sliced

2 cups blueberries

2 peaches, peeled and sliced

2 cups sliced fresh strawberries

1 cup seedless green grapes

1 cup seedless red grapes

1 cup vanilla soy yogurt

2 teaspoons finely chopped nuts

¼ cup raisins

Combine all fruit. Gently stir in yogurt, raisins, and nuts. Add optional toppings, if desired.

Fried Apples

The first time I had fried apples was at a restaurant chain named Cracker Barrel, an adorable country style restaurant and old fashioned store in one. I would indulge in my own makeshift vegetarian platter of fried apples, cheese grits, biscuits, and these cheesy breakfast hash brown casserole they are known for. Ultimately, I had to give up their versions, but I have created by own versions of all of the above. You can add more vegan butter to these to be more indulgent, but I think this is the lowest amount of butter you can use without losing the texture of the original.

5 apples, peeled, cored and sliced (I use Macintosh)

¼ cup vegan butter

¼ cup maple syrup

1 teaspoon cinnamon

1 pinch salt

Melt butter in a medium-sized pan over medium heat. Cook slowly, turning slices as they start to brown. When they are soft on both sides, season with a pinch of salt and the syrup.

Preheat oven to 350°F. Grease a round cake pan and bake apples for 15 minutes. Sprinkle with optional granola for a breakfast, or serve as a side dish breakfast, lunch, or dinner.

Gingered Peaches and Apricots

This is one of those recipes I totally created by mistake. I had multiple recipes going, and I accidentally sprinkled ginger on what was supposed to be a peach and apricot cobbler. Turns out, this was better than the cobbler!

8 peaches, peeled and quartered

1 cup dried apricots

½ cup raisins

½ cup maple syrup

1 teaspoon ground ginger

½ cup granola, optional

chopped nuts, optional

Preheat oven to 350°F. Grease a casserole dish. Place peaches, apricots, and raisins in dish. Combine syrup and ginger; sprinkle over fruit. Bake 20 minutes. Serve warm.

Baked Pears

This is a great Thanksgiving dessert to offset all the heavier food you're likely indulging in. These combined with the fried apples make a wonderful cooked fruit platter or dessert.

4 medium ripe pears

2 tablespoons lemon juice

1/3 cup coarsely chopped walnuts

4 tablespoons rice syrup

¼ teaspoon ground cinnamon

1 tablespoon vegan butter

2/3 cup apple juice

Core and peel pears and brush with some of the lemon juice. Place in a greased 1-quart baking dish.

Preheat oven to 350°F.

In a bowl, combine the walnuts, raisins, syrup, brown sugar, lemon peel, cinnamon and remaining lemon juice. Spoon into pears. Dot with vegan butter. Pour apple juice around pears. Bake, uncovered, for 30-40 minutes, or until pears are tender, basting several times as needed.

Blueberry Parfaits

I never appreciated blueberries until I moved to Kansas. New Jersey, where I was raised, grows a lot of blueberries. Oddly enough, I did not discover this until I left. When they are in season, I buy several cartons of New Jersey organic blueberries and freeze them. This is one of the yummier things I do with the fresh berries.

1 ½ cups blueberries

1 (6 ounce) container vanilla soy yogurt

1 teaspoon flaxseed meal

½ banana, sliced

1/3 cup granola

1 teaspoon rice syrup

Layer ¼ cup blueberries, 1/3 container yogurt, 1/3 teaspoon flaxseed meal, 1/3 of the sliced banana, and about 2 tablespoons of granola in a large bowl. Continue to build the parfait, repeating the layers until all of the ingredients are used completely. Top with the rice syrup.

Frosty Banana Sundaes

Before frozen non-dairy ice cream and treats were readily available, this was my treat. Now, when I have bananas that are getting a bit too ripe, I peel and freeze for this recipe.

4 medium bananas, halved and split

½ cup rice syrup

½ cup vegan chocolate chips

1 cup frozen sliced strawberries

Gather 4 small freezer safe cups or containers. Place one halved sliced banana, ¼ cup strawberries, a spoonful of rice syrup over the fruit, and a sprinkle of the chocolate chips in each container. Cover and freeze. Defrost before eating. Top with optional gluten-free vegan whipped cream, sprinkles, nuts, etc.

Chocolate Covered Strawberries

Who doesn't love these? It's really easy to make. You could just as easily cover other fruits and nuts in addition to, or instead of, strawberries. I really enjoy using a combination of berries, oranges, and nuts to create a gift basket.

1 bag vegan chocolate chips

1 pint regular or long stem strawberries

In a microwave-safe bowl, or in the top of a double boiler over simmering water, cook chocolate until melted. Stir occasionally until chocolate is smooth. Holding berries by the stem, or by holding regular berries with tongs, dip each one in melted chocolate, about three-quarters of the way to the stem. Place on wire rack and chill in refrigerator until hardened.

Papaya Cups

I had never had a papaya until a friend served it to me this way, like a pineapple boat. This is not her recipe, as she used cottage cheese, Jell-O and other products not quite safe for us, but she gave me a great idea nonetheless.

1 cup non-dairy vanilla yogurt

¼ cup walnuts

¼ cup dried mango

1 cup chopped fresh pineapple

2 kiwi, peeled and diced

½ cup red grapes

2 medium papayas, cut in half lengthwise and seeded

2 tablespoons agave nectar or rice syrup

In a bowl, mix the yogurt, walnuts, and mango. Fold in the pineapple. Spoon the mixture into the centers of the papaya halves. Top with kiwi and grapes. Drizzle with sweetener to serve.

Baked Grapefruit

2 large grapefruit, cut in half

½ cup gluten-free oats or granola

1 tablespoon brown sugar

½ teaspoon ground cinnamon

4 teaspoons vegan butter

4 teaspoons shredded coconut

Preheat the oven to 450°F.

Remove all visible seeds from the grapefruit and loosen sections from membrane with a sharp knife. Place grapefruit halves cut side up in a baking dish.

Stir the oats or granola, sweetener, and cinnamon together in a small bowl; add the butter and mash with a fork to incorporate oat or granola mixture into the butter. Spread a quarter of this mixture over the top of each grapefruit half. Sprinkle coconut on top.

Bake until the topping is golden brown, about 10 minutes.

Fig Compote

Guess what? Figs are not just for Newtons but are a wonderful and nutritious fruit you can find year round in the dried fruit aisle. Ideally, get unsulphured figs that have not been sweetened.

1 cup apple juice

¼ cup granulated sweetener

½ teaspoon molasses

¼ cup water

1 tablespoon fresh lemon juice

½ cup dried apricot halves, quartered

½ cup dried whole figs, sliced

½ cup dried cranberries

½ teaspoon ground ginger

¼ teaspoon cinnamon

1 teaspoon vanilla extract

Simmer apple juice, sweetener, molasses, water, and lemon juice in a small bowl, stirring occasionally until dissolved.

Add fruit and seasonings; simmer 5 more minutes or until fruits are plump and liquid is slightly thick. Serve chilled.

Melon Salad

When it's really hot and humid outside, I crave this. Otherwise, I am not much of a melon fan. I will warn you that many cannot have melons combined with other foods, so I would save this for when it can be the main course. I suggest waiting an hour before eating any other non-fruit, or 2 hours after a meal to avoid the sour stomach that melons are renowned to cause.

1 large watermelon

1 cantaloupe, halved and seeded

1 honeydew melon, halved and seeded

2 cups halved fresh strawberries

2 cups seedless grapes

½ cup water

¼ cup granulated sweetener

2 tablespoons grated lemon zest

With a large, sharp knife, remove the top ¼ section of the watermelon. With a melon baller, scoop the inside of watermelon, removing as many seeds as possible. Leave ½ inch of flesh inside the shell of the watermelon. Scoop cantaloupe and honeydew in the same manner. Refrigerate fruits separately until ready to assemble.

In a small saucepan bring water and sweetener to a boil. Remove from heat, and continue stirring until sweetener has dissolved. Add lemon zest, and set aside to cool.

To serve, place fruit in a large bowl. Pour syrup over, and toss thoroughly. Transfer mixture to watermelon bowl, and serve.

Appetizers

As a vegetarian, there were many appetizers available to me. As a gluten-free vegan, not so much, or so I thought. A little creativity and time revealed that there are lots of options available to us.

Peach and Mango Salsa

My former roommate, Cammie, got me hooked on The Newman's version of peach salsa, and we started putting it on everything, including the corn casserole recipe that appears later in this book. Finally, I've come up with my own version. Serve with your own chips or crudités, or be creative and put it on other recipes for added flavor. This salsa is sweet but you really don't quite taste the fruit in it. You just know its not just tomatoes.

1 mango, peeled, seeded and diced

2 peaches, peeled and diced

4 medium tomatoes, diced

¼ cup chopped fresh cilantro

1 clove of garlic, minced

1 teaspoon salt

2 tablespoons fresh lime juice

¼ cup chopped red onion

In a medium bowl, combine the mango, peaches, tomatoes, cilantro, and garlic. Stir in the salt, lime juice, and red onion. To blend the flavors, refrigerate for about 30 minutes before serving.

Cheesy Bean Dip

This is the first of many recipes where I will say that without Daiya, this would not be in this book. Certainly I have no ill will towards the other vegan brands, but they just did not yield the flavor and texture I was after.

1 (16 ounce) can refried beans, or 2 cups your recipe

1 package vegan cream cheese, softened

1 container vegan sour cream

2 cups of salsa, our recipe or your favorite jar salsa

1 large tomato, chopped

1 green bell pepper, chopped

1 bunch chopped green onions

1 small head iceberg lettuce, shredded

1 (6 ounce) can sliced black olives, drained

2 cups shredded vegan cheddar cheese

1 teaspoon each chili and onion powders

Salt and pepper, to taste

In a medium bowl, blend the seasonings and refried beans. Spread the mixture onto a large serving platter. Mix the sour cream and cream cheese in a medium bowl. Spread over the refried beans. Top the layers with salsa. Place a layer of tomato, green bell pepper, green onions and lettuce over the salsa, and top with cheese. Garnish with black olives.

Baked Potato Skins

I am such a fan of potatoes that when I was trying to lose weight ages ago, I would not consider a high-protein diet because I would have to give up potatoes and not because I would have to eat all that meat, which I really do not care for in the least. These are so good and an appetizer you can give everyone and they will never know what's not in them.

4 large baking potatoes, baked

3 tablespoons vegetable oil

1 tablespoon vegan Parmesan cheese

½ teaspoon salt

¼ teaspoon garlic powder

¼ teaspoon paprika

1 ½ cups shredded vegan cheddar cheese

½ cup vegan sour cream

4 green onions, sliced

½ cup broccoli florets, chopped small

Cut potatoes in half lengthwise; scoop out pulp, leaving a 1/4-inch shell (save pulp for another use). Place potatoes skins on a greased baking sheet. Combine oil, Parmesan cheese, broccoli, salt, garlic powder, and paprika; brush over both sides of skins. Bake at 475°F for 7 minutes; turn. Bake until crisp, about 7 minutes more. Sprinkle cheddar cheese inside skins. Bake 2 minutes longer or until the cheese is melted. Top with sour cream and onions. Serve immediately.

Stuffed Mushrooms

This is one of my Thanksgiving staples, and hopefully now one of yours, too.

1 pound large fresh mushrooms

3 tablespoons gluten-free bread crumbs

3 tablespoons vegan sour cream

2 tablespoons vegan parmesan cheese

2 tablespoons chopped chives

2 tablespoons vegan cream cheese

2 teaspoons wheat-free tamari

Preheat oven to the BROIL setting. Remove stems from mushrooms; set caps aside. Chop stems, reserving 1/3 cup. You can save stems for another recipe, like veggie stock, otherwise compost! In a bowl, combine the bread crumbs, sour cream, Parmesan cheese, chives, cream cheese tamari, and reserved mushroom stems; mix well. Place mushroom caps on a baking sheet coated with nonstick cooking spray; stuff with crumb mixture. Place in oven on the closest rack to the heat and broil for 5-7 minutes or until lightly browned.

Hummus

I get these intense hummus cravings from time to time that rival my chocolate cravings. Hummus can be spiced in a number of ways, and any way you serve it, I love it. Try not to omit the tahini. Yes, it's a bit high in fat, but sesame seeds are one of the highest sources of calcium, which is what I think fuels my cravings to begin with. To reduce the overall fat, I reduced the amount of olive oil traditionally used. If fat is not a concern for you, add more of both of these to suit your tastes.

2 cups canned garbanzo beans, rinsed and drained

1/3 cup sesame tahini

¼ cup lemon juice

1 teaspoon salt

1 cloves garlic, minced

1 teaspoon olive oil

1 pinch paprika

1 teaspoon minced fresh parsley

Place the garbanzo beans, tahini, lemon juice, salt, and garlic in a blender or food processor. Blend until smooth. Transfer mixture to a serving bowl. Drizzle olive oil over the garbanzo bean mixture. Sprinkle with paprika and parsley.

Pita Chips

Serve these with our hummus, salsa, or other recipes, or switch it up by removing the pepper and garlic salt and substituting a blend of cinnamon and granulated sweetener of choice. I prefer these really crunchy, but you can bake them less to be softer.

12 gluten-free pita breads

¼ cup olive oil

½ teaspoon black pepper

1 teaspoon garlic salt

Preheat oven to 375°F. Cut each pita into 8 triangles. Place triangles on greased cookie sheet. In a small bowl, combine the oil, pepper, and garlic salt. Feel free to add additional spices, if desired. Brush each triangle with oil mixture. Bake for about 5-7 minutes, or until lightly browned and crispy.

Thai Rice Wraps

When I owned by retail shop in downtown Lawrence, Kansas, I was just a few doors down from a wonderful Thai restaurant. One of my favorites was their Spring Rolls. I've done my best to duplicate them here, and lighten them up as well. These can be a meal in itself for me, especially with my Cold Sesame Noodles and Scallion Pancakes.

2 ounces rice vermicelli

8 rice wrappers (8.5 inch diameter)

4 ounces of firm tofu, drained, cut into matchsticks

2 tablespoons chopped fresh mint leaves

2 leaves of lettuce, any variety, chopped

½ cup shredded carrots

¼ cup water

2 tablespoons fresh lime juice

1 clove garlic, minced

2 tablespoons agave nectar

3 tablespoons gluten free tamari or hoisin sauce

Cook noodles according to package instructions and drain. Fill a large bowl with warm water and dip each wrapper into the hot water briefly to soften. Place a few tofu pieces, a handful of vermicelli, mint, carrot, and lettuce in the center of wrapper, leaving about 2 inches uncovered on each side. Fold uncovered sides inward, then tightly roll the wrapper. Repeat. In a small bowl, mix the water, lime juice, garlic, agave nectar, and hoisin or tamari and use as a dipping sauce. Chill sauce and rolls 30 minutes before serving.

Spinach and Artichoke Dip

Daiya again to the rescue here, with the help of Mimic Crème. You can omit the artichokes if you don't care for them, but they are very high in nutrients and I expect them to be the next "superfood" discovery soon enough.

1 package chopped frozen spinach, thawed
1 can artichoke hearts, chopped
1 container vegan cream cheese
¼ cup plain milk product, or Mimic Crème
4 tablespoons vegan cream cheese
1/3 cup nutritional yeast
¼ cup vegan parmesan cheese
1 cup chopped green onion
¼ cup chopped chives
1 red bell pepper, chopped
2 tablespoons olive oil
½ cup shredded vegan cheddar or mozzarella
1 clove minced garlic

Preheat oven to 350°F. Heat oil in skillet, add peppers and garlic, sauté 4 minutes over medium heat, then add milk, cooking an additional 1-2 minutes. Add chopped artichokes, cream cheese, green onions, and chives, and heat through until melted. Add parmesan, nutritional yeast, ½ of the vegan cheddar and cream cheese in the recipe, and cook until melted. Add spinach, stirring frequently, and let cook for 3-minutes, until mixture begins to thicken. Transfer mix into a casserole or baking dish and top with the rest of the vegan cheese. Bake for 10 minutes, or until the cheese on top melts and the mixture is warm. Serve hot with our pita chips or small slices of gluten-free garlic toast.

Scallion Pancakes

When I first tasted these at a small NJ Chinese restaurant, I could not believe how good they were. They are rare on the menus out here in Kansas, so I created my own, which luckily, were already gluten-free vegan to begin with.

4 pounds of potatoes, peeled and shredded
1 bunch of scallions, sliced thin, both green and white parts
2 tablespoons of flaxmeal mixed with 6 tablespoons of water
1 tablespoon salt
½ teaspoon black pepper
½ cup vegetable oil, for coating

Squeeze the shredded potatoes dry. In a large bowl, using 2 forks, mix the shredded potatoes with the scallions, flax preparation, salt and pepper.

Preheat oven to 400°F. Grease 2 cookie sheets. Press batter into firm cakes and place in a single layer on sheets. Brush with a small amount of oil. You may not use all the oil called for in the recipe. Bake for 10 minutes, gently turn over, brush with oil, and bake another 10-15 minutes or until golden brown. Cut into wedges and serve with applesauce, sour cream, or your favorite dipping sauce.

Veggie Tempura

Just a couple of pieces of this satisfies my craving for fried food. Drain well and serve with a light meal, such as soup and salad.

4-5 assorted vegetables, chopped into equal sizes and patted dry of excess moisture.

Prepare a deep fryer or add 2 inches of oil into a large heavy skillet.

Batter Recipe

¼ cup corn starch
¼ cup sorghum flour
½ cup rice flour
½ teaspoon baking powder
¼ teaspoon salt
Egg replacer for one egg, prepared according to box

Dipping sauce

3 tablespoons **each** water and wheat-free tamari
a dash of rice vinegar
a bit of granulated sweetener

In a large bowl mix together the prepared Egg replacer and 1 cup iced water. Add the dry ingredients and whisk together. When the oil is ready, dip some of the vegetables into the tempura mix, coat on all sides, and carefully place them in the hot oil. Do not overcrowd pan. Cook for 1 minute. If the tops have not cooked, turn the piece over and cook another 20-40 seconds. The breading may not get deep brown. Remove the vegetables and drain on a paper towel.

Cold Noodles with Sesame Sauce

I could eat these every day and not get sick of it. I guess I am just really into Asian foods, but I do think it's the tahini again that does it for me. You can equally use peanut butter, which I often do, if you do not have tahini.

1 (16 ounce) package gluten-free spaghetti or linguini

4 tablespoons of peanut butter **or** sesame tahini

2 cloves garlic, minced

2 tablespoons agave nectar

2 tablespoons tamari

1 teaspoon sesame oil

1 teaspoon ground ginger

1 green onion, chopped

2 teaspoons sesame seeds

a pinch of red pepper flakes, optional

Cook pasta according to package instructions. Drain. Melt the peanut butter in the microwave 15 to 20 seconds. Whisk the honey, tamari, and pepper flakes into the peanut butter, then stir in the sesame oil and ginger. Mix in the garlic and green onions and toss with the noodles. Top with the sesame seeds.

Veggie Quesadillas

If you happen to have one of those electric quesadilla makers like I do, feel free to use it. Otherwise, follow the pan instructions below.

1 tablespoon oil

1 cup thinly sliced mushrooms

1 medium onion, cut into thin wedges

1 green pepper, cut into thin strips

1 garlic clove, minced

4 cups chopped spinach or other greens

4 gluten-free tortillas

1 cup vegan cheddar cheese shredded

Heat oil in skillet over medium high heat until hot. Add mushrooms, onion, pepper, garlic, salt and pepper. Cook and stir until onions and peppers have slightly softened, covering the pan to hasten the process. Reduce heat to low, add spinach leaves. Cook an additional 1 to 2 minutes or until spinach is wilted. Remove from heat. Place 1/4 of the veggie mixture on half of each tortilla. Spread cheese on the other half and fold over. Place onto ungreased cookie sheet and broil until browned. Alternatively you can heat each side of the quesadilla in a pan until browned and cheese melts.

Soups

I love soup. Many are naturally vegan to begin with, so there was not much to modify, and with gluten-free pasta, you will feel satisfied. You can always make up a batch to save for your lunches or freeze for later.

Cheesy Potato Soup

Once again, Daiya steals the show. This used to be my favorite soup before my dairy allergy kicked in, but now, it's back.

1 small onion, chopped

1 clove garlic, minced

3 tablespoons potato flour

1 teaspoon salt

1 teaspoon dried basil

½ teaspoon pepper

3 cups vegetable broth

1 tablespoon oil

2 large baked or boiled potatoes, peeled and cubed

1 cup Mimic Crème or plain milk product

1 teaspoon chives

½ cup shredded vegan cheddar

Sauté onion and garlic in the oil until tender. Stir in flour, chives, salt and pepper; mix well. Gradually add broth. Bring to boil and stir for 2 minutes. Add the potatoes and crème/milk, heating through but do not boil. Garnish with cheese.

Minestrone

Growing up Italian in a mostly Italian town, I had my share of delicious Minestrone. There was one restaurant in particular whose soup was so good that I was devastated when I moved away. That was years ago, and while I am not sure I would remember it if I tasted it, I am very pleased with how this one came out.

2 tablespoons olive oil

1 clove of garlic, chopped

2 medium onions, chopped

2 cups chopped celery

3carrots, sliced

4 cups vegetable broth

4 cups tomato sauce

1 cup canned kidney beans, drained

3 zucchini, diced

1 teaspoon each dried oregano and basil

salt and pepper to taste

½ cup gluten-free small shells or other pasta

In a large stock pot, over medium-low heat, sauté onions, celery, carrots, and garlic for 5 minutes. Add broth, water, and tomato sauce, bring to boil, stirring frequently. Reduce heat to low and add remaining ingredients. Once pasta is cooked the soup is done.

Hot and Sour Soup

I love this soup as an appetizer, especially on a cold snowy day. I prefer mine spicy, but you can make yours as mild as you wish.

1 cup sliced mushrooms, any variety

4 cups vegetable stock

½ cup diced bamboo shoots

1 teaspoon wheat-free tamari

½ teaspoon granulated sugar product

1 teaspoon salt

½ teaspoon ground white pepper

2 tablespoons cornstarch

3 tablespoons water

8 ounces of firm tofu, cubed and drained

2 tablespoons thinly sliced green onion

pinch of red pepper flakes, to taste, optional

Place the mushrooms, stock, and bamboo shoots into a saucepan, bring to a boil, and simmer for 10 minutes. Stir in tamari, sugar, salt, and white pepper. Combine cornstarch with 3 tablespoons water and add to the pan. Heat to boiling, stirring regularly. Add the tofu and cook 1 to 2 minutes. Sprinkle with scallions just before serving.

Peas and Carrots Soup

I was never much of a fan for pea soup's texture until I thought of adding carrots. Feel free to add additional vegetables to your liking. This makes for a nice, thick soup that along with some gluten-free bread, is a great meal.

1 tablespoon vegetable oil

1 medium red onion, chopped

1 clove of garlic, minced

2 cups dried split peas

½ cup uncooked quinoa

1 teaspoon salt

4 cups water

4 cups vegetable broth

3 carrots, chopped

2 stalks of celery, chopped, including leaves

1 cup fresh spinach, leaves only

3 potatoes, diced

½ teaspoon ground black pepper

Sauté onion and garlic for 5 minutes in soup pot. Add the peas, salt, stock, and water. Bring to a boil and reduce heat. Simmer for 2 hours, stirring occasionally. Add remaining ingredients, and simmer for an additional hour, or until the peas and vegetables are tender.

Creamy Mushroom Soup

Better tasting and better for you than the canned version, this soup also doubles as a gravy or topping for potatoes, biscuits, stuffing, or your favorite recipe.

5 cups sliced fresh mushrooms

1 ½ cups vegetable broth

½ cup chopped onion

2 tablespoons vegan butter

3 tablespoons rice flour

¼ teaspoon salt

¼ teaspoon ground black pepper

1 cup Mimic Crème or plain milk product

½ cup frozen peas, defrosted

In a large heavy saucepan, cook mushrooms in the broth with onion until tender, about 10 to 15 minutes. In blender or food processor, puree the mixture, leaving some chunks of vegetable in it. Set aside. In the saucepan, melt the butter, whisk in the flour until smooth. Add the salt, pepper, crème/milk, and vegetable puree. Stirring constantly, bring soup to a boil and cook until thickened.

White Bean and Greens Soup

Traditionally, this recipe calls for dried white beans as well as escarole and chicken broth. If you have the time, please use dried beans made from scratch. However, I actually prefer using canned navy beans for this short-cut method, making the soup quick to make and easy to modify. If you cannot find escarole, or want a change, I highly suggest turnip greens, spinach, or kale, or a combination of all three.

2 cloves garlic, minced

1 medium sweet onion, chopped

2 cans navy beans, drained and rinsed

8 cups vegetable broth

4 cups chopped escarole or other dark leafy greens

Cook onions and garlic in a large pot with a little stock or oil for 5 minutes on medium heat, until tender. Add the rest of the stock, navy beans, and chopped escarole/greens. Cook until the greens are tender, about 3 minutes. Turn off heat and allow the greens to wilt in the broth 15 minutes or more if you have the time. Reheat before serving. If desired, top with gluten-free croutons.

Quick and Easy Soup

Of all my soups, this is my favorite because as the title implies, it's quick, easy, and yet very nutritious. This recipe was inspired by my good friend, Christian, who replied to my Facebook posting "Does anyone have a recipe for turnip greens?" I've modified it so much he probably doesn't even recognize it, but I had to replace the miso and other gluten containing ingredients. Below is my favorite way of making it, but again, feel free to use what you can obtain.

6 cups vegetable stock

6 sun dried tomatoes, sliced into strips

4 ounces of tofu, cubed and drained

2 cups of turnip greens, or other dark leafy greens

¼ package thin rice vermicelli (cellophane) noodles

1 scallion, sliced thinly, both green and white parts

pinch of red pepper flakes, optional

Heat stock and tomatoes, bringing to a boil. Reduce heat and add tofu, turnip greens, and noodles. Cover and turn off heat. Allow to sit 10 minutes. Reheat to a boil, then serve.

Tofu Pho (Vietnamese Noodle Soup)

Even though I am originally from the NYC metro area, I first had this wonderful Vietnamese soup in Kansas at a small Vietnamese restaurant. I fine tuned the recipe to suit my preferences, but I am sure you will find this quite filling and comforting.

4 cups vegetable stock

1 slice ginger root, about ½"

1 teaspoon agave nectar

½ teaspoon hot chili-garlic sauce

1 cup tofu, diced and drained

2 cups sliced mushrooms, any variety

¼ of a package of rice vermicelli noodles

2 green onions, sliced, green and white parts

¼ cup shredded basil

½ cup fresh (mung) bean sprouts

Pour broth into large saucepan cook over high heat. Add ginger, agave nectar, and chili-garlic sauce. Bring to a boil. Simmer over medium-low heat for 10 minutes. Remove and discard ginger.

Meanwhile, cut tofu into cubes. Slice mushrooms. Oil a large frying pan and set over medium-high heat. Add mushrooms and tofu. Cook until tofu begins to brown, about 5 minutes. Add to broth. Bring soup to a boil, then stir in noodles. Boil gently, stirring often, until noodles are tender, 3 to 5 minutes.

Stir in onions and mint, then ladle into soup bowls. Top with bean sprouts.

Cheddar Tortilla Soup

I only really began to enjoy this soup just as my dairy allergy began. The Daiya cheddar really makes this recipe, but if you cannot get Daiya in your area, Follow Your Heart's cheeses will do. Try it with their spicy variety.

2 tablespoons vegetable oil

1 medium sweet onion, chopped

1 green pepper, diced

1 clove of garlic, minced

1 tablespoon ground cumin

1 teaspoon chili powder

1 (28 ounce) can crushed tomatoes, including juice

6 cups vegetable broth

2 cups Mimic Crème or plain milk product

1 can corn, red peppers, and black beans, drained

12 ounces tortilla chips

1 cup shredded vegan Cheddar cheese or nacho cheese

Sauté the peppers, onions, garlic, chili powder, and cumin in the oil 5 minutes, until vegetables are tender. Mix in the tomatoes and juice, broth, and season with salt and pepper. Bring to a boil, then reduce heat to low, and simmer 30 minutes. Add drained Mexicorn and crème/milk into the soup, and continue cooking 5 minutes, until warm. Stir in cheese until melted. Serve and top with chips.

Pasta Fagioli

Here is another childhood favorite. You have a lot of freedom to modify this recipe, so any combination of beans, gluten-free pasta, and veggies will work.

2 tablespoons olive oil

1 medium sweet onion, diced

2 cloves garlic, minced

1 (28 ounce) can tomato sauce

6 cups water or vegetable broth

1 tablespoon dried parsley

1 teaspoon dried basil

1 teaspoon dried oregano

1 teaspoon salt

2 cans white beans, rinsed and drained

¼ cup vegan parmesan cheese

1 pound of any shape small gluten-free pasta

In a large pot over medium heat, cook onion in olive oil until translucent. Stir in garlic and cook until tender. Reduce heat, and stir in tomato sauce, water, parsley, basil, oregano, salt, beans, navy and Parmesan. Simmer 1 hour. Cook pasta according to package instructions. Drain and add to soup. Simmer another 5 minutes before serving.

Chunky Tomato Soup

As a child, one of my favorite lunches was tomato soup and a grilled cheese sandwich. I quickly learned there is a BIG difference between homemade tomato and the condensed stuff in a can, which usually contains flour and other gluten containing ingredients. I like to make a big pot of this and freeze it, and yes, I still have it with vegan grilled cheese.

1 red bell pepper, diced

1 yellow bell pepper, diced

1 teaspoon butter, divided

8 tomatoes, peeled and sliced

1 (28 ounce) can diced tomatoes

1 medium onion, diced

1 clove of garlic, minced

2 cups vegetable broth

1 teaspoon each salt, agave nectar, oregano and basil

1 cup Mimic Crème or plain milk product

1 tablespoon cornstarch

Place the peppers in a large pot with ¼ teaspoon butter, and cook, stirring constantly, until peppers are slightly charred. Mix in tomatoes, canned tomatoes, onion, garlic, and broth. Add seasonings. Bring to a boil, and cook 20 minutes, until tomatoes are soft. In a small pan, heat the milk, butter, and cornstarch until thickened. Mix into the vegetables. Strain about ½ the soup and transfer to a blender. Blend until smooth, and return to the pot. Bring soup to a boil, reduce heat to low, and simmer 5 minutes before serving.

Grandma's Sicilian Soup

My grandmother made this with sausage, and even back then, I picked around the sausage to get at the spinach and potatoes. I'm sure she had another name for this, but I never knew it. My version is way healthier, even with the Mimic Crème.

1 tablespoon vegetable oil

¾ cup diced onion

1 teaspoon minced garlic

4 cups vegetable stock

2 potatoes, halved and sliced

1 bag spinach leaves

pinch of red pepper flakes, optional

½ cup Mimic Crème, or milk product with 1 teaspoon cornstarch, diluted

Heat oil in a large saucepan over medium heat. Sauté onions until translucent; add garlic and cook 1 minute. Stir in broth, water and potatoes; simmer 15 minutes. Reduce heat to low and add spinach and cream; simmer until heated through and serve.

Salads

I used to think that salad was limited to lettuce and tomatoes, as this is the only salad I was ever fed as a child. Then, with the invention of the salad bar, all of that changed. Now, you can make almost anything into a salad, making it an easy way to get lots of vitamins with limited or often no cooking at all. They are portable and great for lunch or dinner on those hot sweltering nights.

Spinach Salad

It took me until fairly recently to appreciate raw spinach for salads, yet cooked spinach is my favorite vegetable. If you prefer, use another salad green, or a mix of spinach and other leafy greens.

½ cup chopped walnuts

1 bag of spinach leaves

2 tomatoes, chopped

½ red onion, thinly sliced

2 tablespoons seedless raspberry jam

2 tablespoons red wine vinegar

2 tablespoons walnut oil

salt and pepper, to taste

In a large bowl, toss together the spinach, walnuts, tomatoes, and red onion.

In a small bowl, whisk together jam, vinegar, oil, pepper, and salt. Pour over the salad just before serving, and toss to coat.

Taco Salad

I used to think that any salad was healthy about 20 years ago, and then I started to do some reading. Taco Salads, with their fried shells, beef, sour cream, cheese, guacamole, and dressing are fat traps disguised with some iceberg lettuce at the bottom. I loved them, but hated the heavy and bloated way I felt afterwards. Now that I "know better" I have created a salad that anyone will enjoy and not regret it.

1 head iceberg or other lettuce, shredded

1 red onion, sliced

1 bunch green onions, chopped, both white and green parts

1 (15 ounce) can black beans, rinsed and drained

1 (15 ounce) can kidney beans, rinsed and drained

2 large tomatoes, chopped

1 green pepper, diced

8 ounces shredded vegan Cheddar cheese

1 (16 ounce) package corn chips, preferably baked (Guiltless Gourmet!)

8 ounces salsa, any variety

½ cup vegan sour cream, if desired

In a large bowl, combine lettuce, red onion, green onion, beans, tomatoes, peppers, and cheese. Mix well. Before serving, add the corn chips. Mix the sour cream and salsa together as a dressing, if desired, or simply top with both. Serve immediately.

Quinoa Salad

Quinoa is a really cool South American grain that is small and round, like couscous, but without the gluten. Of all the grains, it contains the most protein, so I try to use it in everything, instead of rice, in veggie burgers, etc. I make up a large amount and save it for several days.

4 cups quinoa

4 cups water

¼ cup red wine vinegar

2 teaspoons salt

1 teaspoon ground black pepper

4 teaspoons Dijon mustard

¼ cup oil

1 green bell pepper, chopped

½ red onion, chopped

2 tomatoes, chopped

Bring the quinoa and water to a boil in a saucepan. Reduce heat to medium-low, cover, and simmer until the water is absorbed, about 15 to 20 minutes. Refrigerate until cold, about 1 hour.

Place the vinegar, salt, pepper, lemon juice, and mustard into a blender. Drizzle in the oil while blending at high speed until the dressing is thick.

Add the pepper, red onion, and tomatoes to the bowl with the quinoa. Pour the dressing overtop and gently fold until evenly mixed. Best served cold.

Black Beans and Rice Salad

Certainly feel free to use other beans or grains for this recipe. However, I selected black beans because of all the beans, they have the most fiber and nutrients. Plus, I really like black beans. If you are using canned beans, really make sure to rinse and drain them well, or your salad will take on a grayish black color.

2/3 cup uncooked white rice

1 1/3 cups water

1 (15 ounce) can of black beans, drained and rinsed

1 large tomato, diced

¾ cup shredded vegan Cheddar cheese

1/3 cup sliced green onions

1/3 cup vegetable oil

¼ cup balsamic vinegar

½ teaspoon garlic powder

salt and pepper to taste

In a saucepan, bring water to a boil. Add rice and stir. Reduce heat, cover and simmer for 20 minutes. Remove from heat and chill.

In a large bowl, mix together the rice, beans, tomato, cheese, and green onion.

In a small bowl, whisk together the oil, vinegar, peppers, sugar and garlic. Pour over the rice mixture and toss to coat. Cover and refrigerate salad for 30 minutes.

House Salad

Everyone's house salad is different, and so I do my best to get everyone's version when I go out to eat. Mine tend to have an Italian flair, but you can add radishes, raisins, etc to yours.

1 large head romaine lettuce, rinsed, dried, and torn into bite sized pieces

1 large head red leaf lettuce, rinsed, dried, and torn into bite sized pieces

1 (14 ounce) can artichoke hearts, drained and quartered

1 cup sliced red onion

1/3 cup oil

1 cup balsamic vinegar

¼ teaspoon ground black pepper

1/3 cup vegan Parmesan cheese

½ cup chick peas

¼ cup slivered almonds

dash of salt, pepper, and oregano

In a large bowl, combine the romaine lettuce, red leaf lettuce, artichoke hearts, and red onions. Toss together.

Prepare the dressing by whisking together the olive oil, vinegar, salt, pepper, oregano, and cheese. Refrigerate until chilled and pour over salad to coat. Toss and serve. Top with almonds.

Zucchini Salad

Here is another recipe I create completely by mistake, but it's become one of my favorites. I have been asked to take this to a number of BBQ's and other summer events. The longer this is chilled, the better.

6 medium zucchini, diced

1 cup cooked gluten-free elbow or small shell macaroni

½ cup chopped red onion

1 cup chopped sweet red pepper

½ cup chopped green pepper

½ cup corn kernels, drained

Dressing

¾ cup cider vinegar

¼ cup oil

¼ cup agave nectar nectar

½ cup yellow mustard

½ cup sweet relish

salt, pepper, and oregano to taste

In a large bowl, toss together the first six ingredients. In a jar with a tight-fitting lid, combine the salad dressing ingredients; shake well. Pour over salad and toss to coat. Cover and refrigerate for at least 1 hour. Serve with a slotted spoon.

Roasted Vegetable Salad

My very favorite salad, ever. I sometimes top the vegetables on baked potatoes and then have a simple green salad on the side. This is really good with focaccia.

1 eggplant, peeled and sliced into ½ inch pieces

2 large portabella mushrooms, sliced thick

2 cloves garlic, minced

¼ cup olive oil

1 red bell pepper, seeded and sliced into strips

½ red onion, sliced

3 medium zucchini

½ cup balsamic vinegar

¼ cup olive oil

1 tablespoon oregano

salt and pepper to taste

Preheat the oven to 450° F. Grease a large baking sheet.

Spread the veggies in an even layer on the baking sheet. Bake for 15 minutes. Turn and continue to bake another 15 minutes.

While the vegetables roast, whisk together the vinegar, olive oil, and spices in a large serving bowl. Set aside. When the vegetables are slightly toasted, remove from the oven, and place them in the bowl with the dressing. Stir to coat evenly. Taste and adjust salt and pepper if necessary. Chill for a few hours to marinate the vegetables. Serve alone or on top of salad greens.

Potato Salad

I am someone who never liked mayonnaise, so it was not something I had to give up. As such, I created this recipe. True, there are vegan mayos out there, and if you like them, use them as you wish. I personally never tried vegan mayo and feel It's just a food I can live without. You can sub mayo for the sour cream.

5 medium red potatoes

2 tablespoons vegan sour cream

1 tablespoon vegan Parmesan cheese

1 green onion, sliced

2 teaspoons cider vinegar

2 teaspoons Dijon mustard

½ teaspoon salt

¼ teaspoon pepper

Place potatoes in a large saucepan and cover with warm. Bring to a boil. Reduce heat; cover and simmer for 20 minutes or until tender.

In a large bowl, combine the remaining ingredients. Drain potatoes and cut into cubes; add to the mayonnaise mixture and gently toss to coat. Serve immediately.

Broccoli Salad

I don't typically enjoy raw broccoli, but this recipe is a favorite.

2 large broccoli bunches, florets only

1 cup shredded carrots

1 cup shredded broccoli slaw (found in bags or shred the stalks)

1 red onion

¼ cup sliced almonds

1 tablespoon agave nectar or other liquid sweetener

½ cup balsamic vinegar

2 tablespoons olive oil

1 tablespoon vegan parmesan

Cut the broccoli into bite-size pieces and cut the onion into thin bite-size slices. Combine with the slaw and nuts and mix well.

To prepare the dressing, mix the sweetener, oil, cheese, and vinegar together until smooth. Stir into the salad, let chill and serve.

Asian Salad

You can add those canned mandarins or oranges to this recipe if you would like. I myself try not to have too much fruit with other food, as I have a fussy tummy, but they taste really good in this recipe.

6 ounces thin rice noodles, crushed

¼ cup slivered almonds

2 teaspoons sesame seeds

¼ cup vegan butter, melted

1 head napa cabbage, shredded

1 bunch green onions, chopped

¼ cup oil

½ cup rice or balsamic vinegar

1 tablespoon agave nectar

2 tablespoons tamari

Prepare vegetables and place in a large bowl. Make dressing by melting the vegan butter, then adding to it the oil, vinegar, agave nectar, and tamari. Pour over salad and serve immediately.

Tomato Salad

Growing up in the Garden State, really large ripe tomatoes were easy to come by. As such, I became very creative with tomatoes. This is really good with some toasted kalamata olive bread and Minestrone soup.

4 large ripe red tomatoes, sliced

1 cup artichoke hearts, in water, rinsed and drained

10 fresh basil leaves, chopped

½ cup red onion, sliced into thin rings

10 kalamata olives

¼ cup olive oil

½ cup balsamic vinegar

salt and pepper to taste

½ teaspoon oregano

¼ cup vegan parmesan

Alternate and overlap the tomato slices, artichokes, and onion slices on a platter. Sprinkle the basil over the top. Scatter the olives over the salad. Prepare dressing by combining the oil and vinegar, and season with salt, pepper, and oregano. Allow to sit at room temperature 15 minutes before serving. Top with olives and parmesan before serving.

Greek Salad

I like having this salad with hummus and naan as a lunch or light dinner.

1 head of romaine, broken into bite sized pieces

3 large ripe tomatoes, chopped

2 cucumbers, peeled and chopped

1 small red onion, chopped

¼ cup olive oil

4 teaspoons lemon juice

1½ teaspoons dried oregano

salt and pepper to taste

1 cup cubed marinated tofu

6 black Greek olives, pitted and sliced

Drain and press tofu to remove excess liquid. Cut tofu into small cubes. Measure out 1 cup of cubes and place in a bowl. Prepare the dressing by combining the oil, lemon juice, salt, pepper, and oregano and add to tofu. Refrigerate at least 30 minutes.

In shallow salad bowl, or on serving platter, combine salad ingredients. Top with marinated tofu and serve.

Breads

I never tried to make homemade bread until after I had to go gluten-free. I was not thrilled at spending $6 dollars or more for rolls or a loaf of bread that was gummy, chalky, or in some way inferior. These were my best creations. If you are new to breads, be patient and substitute other flours until you find blends you really like.

Focaccia

A thick, seasoned bread that doubles as a pan pizza crust.

Whisk together:

1 cup sorghum flour
1 cup tapioca starch
½ cup potato flour
2 teaspoons xanthan gum
1 ¼ teaspoons sea salt
1 teaspoon dried minced onion
½ teaspoon garlic powder
2 teaspoons dried oregano
2 teaspoons dried basil

Prepare in a glass bowl or measuring cup

Add 1 tablespoon active dry yeast:
1 ¼ cups water at 110°F
A pinch of granulated sweetener

When the yeast is ready, pour the mixture into the dry ingredients and add:

4 tablespoons extra virgin olive oil
1 tablespoon agave nectar
1/2 teaspoon o lemon juice
Egg replacer for 1 egg prepared according to box instructions

Stir to combine. The dough should be sticky and resemble muffin batter, not dough. Dust a round pan with cornmeal and add focaccia. Wet your hand and shape into a rounded loaf. Place the pan into the warm oven and allow it to rise for 20 minutes. Preheat oven to 375°F and bake 25 minutes.

Chapati

Chapatis are thin, flat breads that are eaten much like what we know in the US as wraps. Use for sandwiches, burritos, etc.

1 cup amaranth flour
½ cup millet flour
½ cup sorghum flour
½ cup tapioca starch
2 teaspoons xanthan gum
1 teaspoon salt
1 teaspoon baking powder

Add in:
3 tablespoons olive oil
1 tablespoon agave nectar
Egg replacer for 2 eggs whisked with 4 tablespoons hot water
1 ½ cups hot water
½ cup milk product

Beat the wet ingredients into the dry mix until the batter is smooth. It should look and feel like a thick pancake batter. This may take several minutes.

Heat a lightly oiled/ non-stick spray coated skillet or pancake griddle over medium high heat. When a drop of water sizzles and bounces off the surface, your pan is ready.

Place a large spoonful of batter into the pan and quickly spread the batter out as thin as you can. Let the chapati cook for a minute, or until firm. Flip over and cook the other side for a minute or until done. Repeat until batter is gone.

Multigrain Baguette

When I take the time to make this, it's my favorite bread for roast vegetable sandwiches.

2/3 cup sorghum flour
1/3 cup amaranth flour
½ cup millet flour
1 cup tapioca starch
2 teaspoons xanthan gum
1 ¼ teaspoon salt
2 teaspoons dry egg replacer
Sesame seeds for the top

Prepare the yeast by adding 1 tablespoon instant dry yeast or rapid yeast to 1 ¼ cups water at 110°F, then add 1 teaspoon of any sweetener, granulated or liquid. Wait 10 minutes for the yeast to proof.

Mix together the yeast mix with 4 tablespoons extra virgin olive oil
3 tablespoons agave nectar
½ teaspoon cider vinegar

Gently combine the dry and liquid ingredients. Knead the dough by either using a bread machine, a kitchen aid, or simply by hand. After 3 minutes, let dough rest 1 hour for rapid yeast and up to 2 hours for regular rise.

Punch down the dough and shape into a baguette. Sprinkle sesame and any other seeds/spices on top. Allow loaf to rise a second time, about 2 hours.

Preheat oven to 350°F. Grease a cookie sheet and place bread in center. Bake 30 minutes. It should sound hollow when done.

Naan

An Indian flatbread, much like pita, bit shaped more oblong, like a wrapper.

½ cup water
2 teaspoons granulated sweetener
2 teaspoons active dry yeast
2 cups brown rice flour
½ cup potato starch
½ teaspoon salt
1 teaspoon baking powder
1 teaspoon xanthan gum
2 teaspoons vegetable oil
½ cup plain soy yogurt
Egg replacer for one egg, prepared according to instructions
extra flour for flouring the surface

Preheat the oven to 450°F. Place a heavy baking tray or pizza stone in the oven to heat while you prepare the ingredients.

In a measuring bowl or cup, mix water with 1 teaspoon of the sweetener and the yeast. Allow to sit in a warm place while you prep the rest of the ingredients.

Combine the flour, starch, salt, baking powder, and xanthan in a medium bowl. Add the remaining sweetener, oil, yogurt, egg replacer, and the water/yeast mixture. Blend until smooth. It will be very thick.

Divide the dough into six equal portions. Sprinkle some flour onto your rolling surface or use your hands to press the dough into a pita shape. Roll the dough until it is about ¼ " thick. Sprinkle more flour as needed onto the dough and/or the rolling pin to keep it from sticking.

When you are ready to bake, carefully place each piece of dough onto your baking pan or stone. Bake for 6 minutes, flip over and bake for another 4-6 minutes until they are very browned.

Dinner Rolls

It's amazing how as soon as you think you cannot have something, you miss it, even if you really never ate it much before. That's my relationship with these. Now I like these better than traditional white rolls. **Makes 12 rolls**

1 cup brown rice flour
¾ cup tapioca starch
1/3 cup millet flour
2/3 cup sorghum flour
1 tablespoon potato flour
2 tablespoons granulated sweetener
2 teaspoons xanthan gum
1 teaspoon salt
1 package active dry yeast
½ teaspoon sure-jell/fruit pectin (this is vegan, gelatin is not)
¼ teaspoon agar powder
Egg replacer for 2 eggs, prepared according to package instructions
1 ½ cups warm water at 110°F
1 tablespoon vegan sour cream
2 tablespoons oil

Heat oven to 200°F for five minutes, then shut off. Spray muffin tin with non-stick spray. Place all dry ingredients other than egg replacer, yeast, sure-jell, and agar powder in a medium bowl and blend well.

Place egg replacer, warm water, sour cream, and oil in a bowl and mix until blended by hand or with an electric mixer. Slowly add dry ingredients. If using a mixer, increase speed to medium for 4 minutes.

Divide dough into 12 equal portions and place one into each muffin cup. Cover the muffin tin and place in oven to rise for 20 minutes. When they've risen, remove from oven and preheat oven to 375°F. Place muffin tin back into oven and bake for 20 minutes, until golden.

Kalamata Olive Loaf

A local bakery makes a famous Olive loaf, and I had theirs in mind.

½ cup amaranth flour
½ cup garbanzo flour
½ cup sorghum flour
1/3 cup tapioca starch
2 tablespoons flax seed meal
3 teaspoons xanthan gum
½ cup pitted kalamata olives, chopped roughly
2 teaspoons active dry yeast
1 teaspoon salt
Egg replacer for 2 eggs, prepared according to instructions
¾ cup water, room temperature
5 tablespoons extra virgin olive oil
2 teaspoons agave nectar
2 teaspoons apple cider vinegar

Preheat the oven to 200°F. Add the flours, yeast, and all other dry ingredients other than salt into a medium bowl. Stir in flax meal and combine.

Combine wet ingredients, including the prepared egg replacer, using a hand-mixer or stir by hand. When fully combined, add olives. Slowly add dry ingredient mixture and mix with a wooden spoon until fully blended without lumps. Try not to break the olives as you stir.

Grease a loaf pan and pour the dough into the pan. Use a spatula or knife to evenly shape the top of the loaf. Turn off the oven and place loaf inside. Allow the dough to rise for 90 minutes. It should rise to the very top of the pan.

Increase heat to 350°F and bake for approximately 40 minutes. The crust should be golden. Allow to cool slightly before removing it from the pan to finish cooling.

Irish Soda Bread

This is one of those recipes I did not miss until I had to go gluten-free. I like this one better.

Whisk dry ingredients:

1 cup garbanzo flour
½ cup sorghum flour
½ cup potato starch
2 tablespoons granulated sugar product
1 teaspoon baking soda
1 ½ teaspoons baking powder
1 teaspoon salt
2 teaspoons xanthan gum

Wet Ingredients:

4 tablespoons vegan butter
3/4 cup plain milk product with ½ teaspoon lemon juice
1 tablespoon egg replacer made with ¼ cup warm water
1 tablespoon agave nectar
1 cup raisins

Preheat oven to 375° F. Lightly grease a round cake pan and dust it with flour. Whisk the dry ingredients together in a large mixing bowl. Cut in the shortening.

Whisk the wet ingredients together in a separate bowl. Make a well in the center of the dry ingredients and slowly pour the wet into the dry ingredients. Add raisins. Place dough into the pan and wet your hands to shape the dough into a round loaf.

Bake 30 minutes, until the loaf is golden and crusty and sounds hollow when thumped.

Pizza Dough

In a measuring cup, combine:

1 cup of water at 110°F
1 package dry, active yeast
1 tablespoon granulated sweetener

Whisk together in a bowl and let it sit for 10 minutes or until it begins to foam.

In a large bowl, combine:

2 tablespoons olive oil
1 teaspoon each or dried basil, oregano, and parsley
2 teaspoons apple cider vinegar
1 teaspoon salt
½ teaspoon xanthan gum
Add to the yeast mixture. Then stir in 2 ½ cups gluten-free all-purpose flour.

Knead dough by hand for a few minutes. Oil a pan and sprinkle cornmeal on it to prevent dough from sticking. Shape dough to desired shape of crust round, square, or mini, and let sit 20 minutes.

Preheat oven to 425°F. Bake the crust for 10 minutes. Remove from oven and add your sauce, vegan cheese, veggies, or any other desired toppings. Return to oven and bake another 10 minutes, or until cheese is melted and hot.

Breadsticks

This recipe doubles for hot pretzels. Just shape and bake, adding optional kosher salt on top popping into the oven.

½ cup amaranth flour
¾ cup garbanzo flour
1/3 cup tapioca starch
2 tablespoons granulated sweetener
1 single package quick-rise dry yeast
1 teaspoon xanthan gum
½ teaspoon garlic powder
½ teaspoon salt
1 teaspoon olive oil

Mix together all dry ingredients. Stir in oil and ¾ cup warm water at 110°F. Beat dough with electric mixer on high speed 2 minutes, or by hand, until smooth.

Transfer dough to a large plastic bag with 1 corner snipped off to serve as a pastry bag. Squeeze bag to create 12 breadsticks of equal size. Cover and let rise for 30 minutes, or until breadsticks have doubled in size.

Preheat oven to 400°F. Bake 20 minutes, or until dark golden brown all over and crisp on bottom. Serve immediately.

Sandwich bread

Combine the following:

2/3 cup garbanzo flour
1/3 cup sorghum flour
½ cup tapioca starch
1 cup potato flour
2 teaspoons xanthan gum
1 ¼ teaspoons salt
2 teaspoons dry egg replacer

Prepare the yeast by adding 1 teaspoon granulated sweetener to 1 tablespoon instant dry yeast- or rapid yeast to 1 ¼ cups warm water at 110°F. Wait 10 minutes until it foams before proceeding.

Pour the liquid ingredients into the dry mix. Add:
3 tablespoons oil
3 tablespoons agave nectar
½ teaspoon cider vinegar

Stir to combine ingredients, then knead for a few minutes. Allow to rise 1 hour for rapid yeast and up to 2 hours for regular rise.

After waiting the 1-2 hours, shape dough into loaf shape and add to a greased loaf pan. Allow a second rising time, another 1-2 hours. Dough should rise to the edges of the pan.

Preheat oven to 350°F. Bake 30 minutes, or until loaf begins to brown. You can test with a toothpick, but also tap the loaf. It should sound hollow when done.

Unrye bread

I was never a fan of white bread, and even as a child, I preferred wheat and rye. This was one of the hardest bread product to find a substitute that worked for me. If you were a rye fan like me, it's worth the time to try this one.

In a large bowl, combine:

½ cup sorghum flour
1 cup garbanzo starch
1 cup potato flour
2 teaspoons xanthan gum
1 ¼ teaspoons salt
2 tablespoons unsweetened cocoa powder
2 teaspoons caraway seeds
1 teaspoon minced dried onion

In a separate smaller bowl, prepare your yeast by adding 1 tablespoon active dry yeast to 1 ¼ cups warm water at 110°F and a teaspoon of granulated or liquid sweetener. Allow the yeast to foam, about 10 minutes or so.

When the yeast is ready add:

3 tablespoons oil
1 teaspoon cider vinegar
2 tablespoons molasses
1 egg replacer portion for one egg, prepared according to package instructions

Pour this blend into the flour mixture and stir until a dough forms. Knead by hand or use a bread machine or mixer for 2-3 minutes. If the dough seems dry add more warm water a tablespoon at a time. Cover and allow to sit 2 hours to rise.

After rising, punch down dough and knead again. Shape into the type of loaf you want and allow a second rising time, up to 2 hours, or until the bread approximately doubles in size. Preheat oven to 350°F. Grease the appropriate pan and place dough inside. Bake 30 minutes, and test for doneness by thumping the loaf. It should sound hollow when done.

Oat Bread

Once again, you can substitute quinoa flour if needed

1 ½ cups gluten-free oat flour

¾ cup millet flour

½ cup potato starch

1/3 cup cornstarch

1/3 cup rice flour

¼ flax seed meal

1 tablespoon xanthan gum

Egg replacer for 3 eggs, prepared according to box instructions

1 teaspoon apple cider vinegar

1 packet active dry yeast

1 teaspoon granulated sweetener for proofing yeast

1 tablespoon molasses

3 tablespoons agave nectar

1 ½ teaspoons salt

4 tablespoons melted vegan butter

1 ¼ cups water at 110°F

Grease the bottom of a 10 inch loaf pan. Heat the oven to 200°F and then turn off. In the bowl of your stand mixer sift together the dry ingredients. In a separate medium bowl, mix egg replacer, molasses, vinegar, and melted butter together. Heat your water for preparing the yeast.

Stir together yeast and one teaspoon of sweetener. Add ¼ cup of the water to the yeast mixture. Let the yeast sit for 10 minutes. Once your yeast is ready, add the egg mixture to the dry ingredients, then add the yeast mixture. Slowly add your water to achieve the right consistency. The dough should be like very stiff cake batter. Put the dough in your pan and place in oven to rise for about 2 hours. Once the dough has risen to the top of the pan, bake the bread for 40 minutes at 350°F.

Pasta

What is there to say other than I love pasta as a meal over anything else. However, once gluten issues surfaced, I was really at a loss. I learned that some types of pasta (corn, quinoa, rice) work better in some recipes than others. Luckily, since finding some good cheese and cream replacements, most of my favorite recipes are back on the menu.

Creamy Macaroni and Cheese

Every cookbook author has one recipe that got them started, and for me, it was this one. When the reality of gluten-free vegan set in, I realized this was the meal I would miss above all others. Whether served as a main course or side dish, it really hits the spot. This recipe and its photo won the Daiya cheese contest in June 2010, and my photo was on their website.

8 ounces of gluten-free pasta, any shape
3 cups shredded Vegan Cheddar Cheese
2 tablespoons vegan butter
2 cups unsweetened milk product, or Mimic Crème
2 tablespoons nutritional yeast
¼ teaspoon black pepper
¼ teaspoon paprika
¼ cup vegan parmesan cheese
½ cup gluten-free bread crumbs

Preheat oven to 350°F. Cook pasta for only half of the time listed in the instructions or it will fall apart when you bake it. Drain pasta and set aside. In a saucepan, melt butter. Add milk product and half of the cheddar and cook on low-medium heat until melted, stirring frequently. When melted, add pepper and nutritional yeast. Pour over the macaroni and mix together. Transfer macaroni to a greased 8x8 baking pan or casserole dish. Stir in remaining cheddar. Top with bread crumbs and bake for 30 minutes uncovered, or until the cheese is bubbling and top is starting to brown. Remove from oven and top with the parmesan.

Fettuccine with Mushrooms and Broccoli

Ok, so there is nothing truly "virtuous" about this dish when it comes to fat and calories, but it is compared to the original. I suggest using this as a side dish, and offsetting the high caloric intake with a large dinner salad.

1 pound gluten-free fettuccine or other pasta

1 cup vegan butter

2 cups of Mimic Crème or unflavored milk product

1 teaspoon of nutritional yeast

1 package of vegan cream cheese

1 ¼ cups vegan parmesan cheese

½ cup vegan sour cream

1 cup vegan mozzarella

1 cup sliced mini portabella mushrooms

1 cup broccoli florets, cut small

Bring a large pot of water to a boil. Add fettuccine and cook according to package instructions, adding broccoli florets during the final minute of cooking. Drain. While pasta is cooking, prepare the sauce. In a large saucepan, melt butter into crème/milk product over low heat. Add mushrooms and simmer 5 minutes. Stir in cheeses over medium heat until melted. Stir in the sour cream and heat until warm. Add pasta to sauce. Serve immediately.

Spaghetti with Unmeatballs

There are a number of great vegan meatballs on the market, but I have yet to find a mass produced gluten-free vegan meatball, so here's mine.

1 pound gluten-free spaghetti
1 jar of spaghetti sauce of choice, or your own recipe
1 pound brown lentils
2 cups brown rice
1 medium onion, chopped fine
1 celery stalk, chopped fine
1 teaspoon of parsley flakes
8 cups lower sodium vegetable broth

Bring broth to a boil, then reduce heat and cover pot. Add lentils and rice and simmer until both are cooked, about 40-45 minutes. Check the liquid frequently and add more water or broth if necessary. When ready, add half of the mixture to a food processor and process into a pulp. Remove and combine the rest of the mixture in a large bowl. Add:

1 clove of minced garlic
2 cups milk product
½ cup vegan parmesan cheese
1 teaspoon each dried oregano and basil flakes

Preheat oven to 350°F. Grease a cookie sheet. Shape mixture into balls, about the size of a golf ball. You can cook the entire mix now or shape and freeze the uncooked extras. Place on sheet in center rack of oven and bake 15 minutes, or until they reach the desired color and consistency.

While they are baking, cook your spaghetti according to package instructions and heat your sauce on low until everything is done. Serve with one of our breads and optional vegan parmesan cheese.

Pasta with Pink Sauce

Another rich recipe, but a crowd pleaser. Once again, I suggest serving as a side dish along with my house salad and my chunky tomato soup, or reserve this one for holidays.

1 package gluten-free pasta (I use penne)

5 tablespoons vegan butter

2 cloves minced garlic

2 (28 ounce) cans crushed tomatoes, including juice

1 cup vegan mozzarella cheese, shredded

3 cups Mimic Crème or other milk product

½ cup vegan parmesan

1 cup unmeatball mix, crumbled and cooked, optional

Cook pasta according to package instructions. In a large skillet, sauté garlic in the butter. Add cream/milk and cook for 3 minutes. If desired, add unmeatball crumbles, and heat mixture just until warm, stirring frequently to prevent sticking. Pour in tomatoes and cheese, cooking until cheese melts. Mix sauce into hot pasta. Top with vegan parmesan.

Spicy Pesto Pasta with Tofu

I normally do not care for pesto, but something about the added tofu in this dish seems to really work for me.

1 (16 ounce) package uncooked bowtie or other gluten-free pasta

3 tablespoons olive oil

1 tablespoon hot chili paste

1 pound extra firm tofu, drained, and cut into 1 inch pieces

6 tablespoons prepared basil pesto

½ cup vegan Parmesan cheese

Bring a large pot of water to a boil. Place pasta in the pot, cook for 8 to 10 minutes, until al dente, and drain. Heat the olive oil in a large skillet over low heat. Mix in the chili paste and tofu. Cook and stir frequently, 3-5 minutes, until it begins to brown. Toss the cooked pasta, pesto, and Parmesan cheese into the skillet, and continue cooking just until heated through.

Cheesy Vegetable Lasagna

You can either make traditional layered lasagna, or roll-ups. Either way, this is one of my favorite meals by far, feeds a crowd, and freezes well.

1 (16 ounce) package gluten-free lasagna noodles

1 pound fresh mushrooms, sliced

¾ cup chopped green bell pepper

¾ cup chopped onion

3 cloves garlic, minced

2 tablespoons vegetable oil

2 jars pasta sauce

1 teaspoon dried basil

1 pound of firm tofu, drained and mashed

4 cups shredded vegan mozzarella cheese

½ cup vegan Parmesan cheese

Cook the lasagna noodles in a large pot of boiling water for 10 minutes, or until al dente. Rinse with cold water, and drain. In a large saucepan, cook and stir mushrooms, green peppers, onion, and garlic in oil. Stir in pasta sauce and basil; bring to a boil. Reduce heat, and simmer 15 minutes. Mix together the tofu and 2 cups mozzarella cheese. Set aside. Preheat oven to 350°F.

For traditional lasagna

Spread 1 cup tomato sauce into the bottom of a greased 9x13 inch baking dish. Layer ½ each, lasagna noodles, tofu mix, sauce, and Parmesan cheese. Repeat layering, and top with remaining 2 cups mozzarella cheese. Bake, uncovered, for 40 minutes. Let stand 15 minutes before serving.

For Roll Ups

Coat bottom of pan with tomato sauce. Spread each cooked lasagna noodle with a heaping ¼ cup of tofu mixture. Sprinkle with mozzarella and roll up firmly. Place rolls seam side down into pan, and cover generously with tomato sauce. Top with more mozzarella and parmesan. Bake for 15 minutes.

Pasta Pomodoro

Everyone loves when I make this dish because it's very simple and versatile. It reheats really well for leftovers the next day, and can also be a great side dish for a vegetable main course meal.

1 pound gluten-free angel hair pasta

¼ cup olive oil

½ medium onion, chopped

4 cloves garlic, minced

2 cups roma (plum) tomatoes, diced

1 (28 ounce) can of diced tomatoes

2 tablespoons wheat-free tamari

1 cup of low-sodium vegetable broth

crushed red pepper, optional

2 tablespoons chopped fresh basil

¼ cup vegan parmesan cheese

Cook pasta according to package instructions. Sauté onions and garlic in oil until lightly browned. Reduce heat and add tomatoes, canned tomatoes, tamari and broth; simmer for about 8 minutes. Stir in red pepper, black pepper, basil, and cooked pasta, tossing thoroughly with sauce. Simmer for about 5 more minutes and serve topped with parmesan cheese.

Fiesta Pasta

I like to serve this with taco salad or my homemade salsa and chips. This recipe reheats well and makes a great lunch the next day, or as a side dish to my spinach and cheese enchiladas.

8 ounces gluten-free rotini pasta

1 can kidney beans, rinsed and drained

1 small onion, diced

1 small green pepper, diced

½ cup sliced black olives

1 jar spaghetti sauce

1 teaspoon of chili powder

1 cup shredded vegan cheddar cheese

Preheat oven to 350°F. Cook pasta according to package instructions. Drain. In a medium skillet over medium-high heat, cook beans, peppers, and onions until onion is brown. Combine this mixture with spaghetti sauce, olives, chili powder, and cooked pasta and pour into a 9x13 inch baking dish. Top with cheese. Bake in preheated oven for 30 minutes, until cheese is melted and golden.

Pasta Primavera

You can substitute other seasonal vegetables into this pasta dish instead of what I suggest here.

1 package gluten-free penne pasta

1 yellow squash, chopped

1 zucchini, chopped

1 carrot, cut into matchsticks

½ red bell pepper, cut into matchsticks

½ pint grape tomatoes

5 spears asparagus, trimmed and cut into 1 inch pieces

¼ cup olive oil, divided

¼ teaspoon each salt and pepper

1 tablespoon vegan butter

2 cloves of garlic, minced

1/3 cup chopped fresh parsley

3 tablespoons wheat free tamari

Preheat oven to 450°F. Cook pasta according to package instructions. In a bowl, toss vegetables with 2 tablespoons olive oil, salt and pepper. Arrange vegetables on a baking sheet, and roast 15 minutes. Heat remaining olive oil and butter in a large skillet. Stir in the garlic, and mix in cooked pasta, parsley, and tamari. Gently toss and cook until heated through.

Stuffed Shells

Once I discovered they actually make gluten-free shells, I knew that I would be ok with this way of eating. Then, when I found Daiya, I knew I could make these again.

1 pound package jumbo gluten-free shells

1/3 cup grated carrot

¼ cup shredded zucchini

3 tablespoons chopped onion

1 pound firm tofu, drained and mashed

1 cup shredded mozzarella cheese, divided

½ teaspoon each salt and pepper

1 can of diced tomatoes

1/3 cup tomato paste

1 teaspoon each dried basil, oregano, and minced garlic

Preheat oven to 350°F. Cook pasta according to package instructions. Meanwhile, in a small saucepan over medium heat combine carrot, zucchini and onion. Pour in just enough water to cover; cook until tender and drain. In a large bowl, mash the tofu with a fork. Stir in carrot mixture, cheese, salt and pepper. Mix well and set aside. In a medium saucepan over medium-high heat, combine tomatoes, tomato paste, basil, oregano, and garlic. Bring to a boil; reduce heat to low and simmer for 10 minutes. Stuff each cooked pasta shell with about 1 rounded tablespoon of the filling. Place shells in an ungreased 2-quart baking dish. Pour sauce over shells. Cover and bake in preheated oven for 25 minutes, or until heated through.

Tofu Tetrazzini

Way back in the day when I used to still eat poultry, I had a delicious turkey tetrazzini recipe. Now, I actually like tofu better, believe it or not, and I think the recipe is better than the original.

1 (8 ounce) package gluten-free spaghetti, broken into pieces

¼ cup vegan butter

¼ cup gluten-free all-purpose flour

½ teaspoon salt

¼ teaspoon black pepper

1 cup vegetable broth

1 cup plain milk product or Mimic Crème

½ pound sliced mushrooms

½ cup peas, frozen, defrosted

2 cups chopped cooked tofu

½ cup vegan Parmesan cheese

Preheat oven to 350°F. Lightly grease a 9x13 inch baking dish. Bring a large pot of lightly salted water to a boil. Cook spaghetti according to package instructions. Meanwhile, in a large saucepan, melt butter over low heat. Stir in flour, salt, and pepper. Cook, stirring until smooth. Remove from heat, and gradually stir in broth and cream. Return to heat, and bring to a low boil for 1 minute, stirring constantly. Stir in cooked spaghetti, mushrooms, peas, and tofu. Pour mixture into the prepared baking dish, and top with cheese. Bake 30 minutes in the preheated oven, until bubbly and lightly browned.

Beans

For any of these recipes, you can use either dried beans that you soak and boil until tender, or use canned beans that are well rinsed and drained. There are so many types of beans available that you are not limited to the ones that I feature in a specific recipe.

Boston Baked Beans

I took my husband's famous recipe and completely redid it, so he probably has no idea that this was based on his baked beans.

2 cans of navy beans, rinsed and drained

1 onion, finely diced

2 tablespoons molasses

2 teaspoons salt

¼ teaspoon ground black pepper

½ teaspoon spicy mustard

½ cup gluten-free barbeque sauce

¼ cup agave nectar

Preheat oven to 325°F. Arrange the beans in a casserole dish and layer them with onions. In a saucepan, combine molasses, salt, pepper, mustard, barbeque sauce, tamari, and agave nectar. Bring the mixture to a boil and pour over beans. Cover the dish with a lid or aluminum foil.

Bake for 2 hours, or until beans are really tender. The cooking time varies greatly on this recipe, so check beans often for doneness. Remove the foil about halfway through cooking, and add some water if needed.

Chili

Everybody like Chili, but everyone likes it in their own way. I serve mine over brown rice or baked potatoes with some Daiya cheese.

6 cups of tomato juice or vegetable stock

1 (28 ounce) can tomato sauce

1 (28 ounce) can diced tomatoes

1 ½ cups chopped onion

¼ cup chili powder

2 teaspoons ground cumin

1 ½ teaspoons garlic powder

1 teaspoon salt

1 teaspoon paprika

½ teaspoon ground black pepper

½ teaspoon dried oregano

1 teaspoon agave nectar

2 cans each kidney and black beans, drained and rinsed

Add all ingredients to a large kettle. Bring to boil. Reduce heat and simmer for 1 hour, stirring occasionally. Top with optional shredded vegan cheddar and sour cream, if desired.

Lentil Rice Loaf

One of the first vegetarian frozen meals I found many years ago was a lentil rice loaf, and I thought it was the greatest thing. That company is no longer in business, but I have done the best I can to duplicate the recipe. I use leftovers in sandwiches, but sometimes I also take the uncooked mix and bake into meatballs.

½ cup walnuts
2 tablespoons olive oil
1 onion, diced fine
1 large carrot, peeled and grated
1 cup mushrooms, diced fine
2 cups cooked lentils
1 cup cooked brown rice
¼ to ½ cup vegetable broth, as needed
3 tablespoons potato flour
1 teaspoon dried basil
¼ teaspoon dried oregano
2 tablespoons ketchup
black pepper, to taste
2 tablespoons of tamari

Preheat the oven to 350°F. Spray a loaf pan with nonstick spray and set aside. Grind the walnuts into a coarse meal using a food processor. Place in a large mixing bowl and set aside.

Sauté vegetables in the oil until soft. Add to the bowl along with all the remaining ingredients. Mash all ingredients, adding only as much liquid as needed to create a soft, moist loaf that holds together and is not runny. Press mixture into the prepared pan and bake for 45 minutes to 1 hour, or until cooked through.

Let the loaf cool in the pan for 10 to 15 minutes, then turn out onto a plate or platter and slice.

Garbanzos Alà King

This was one of my first vegetarian recipes I created years ago, right out of college. Even "veganized" its one of my favorites, easy to make, and everyone loves it.

1 cup sliced mushrooms
½ cup red bell pepper, chopped
½ cup potato flour
½ cup nutritional yeast flakes
½ teaspoon salt
½ teaspoon paprika
2 cups plain milk product
1 can of chick peas, rinsed and drained
½ cup scallions, green and white part, finely chopped

Sauté the mushrooms and peppers in a small amount of oil or nonstick spray for 3-4 minutes, stirring frequently. Stir in the flour, then add nutritional yeast and spices and continue cooking and stirring for another minute, just to warm the mixture.

Remove from heat and gradually stir in the milk, mixing constantly to avoid lumps. Return to heat and continue cooking. Stir constantly until thickened, then add chickpeas and scallions, and continue cooking another 3-5 minutes or until the chickpeas are thoroughly warmed.

Serve at once over rice, quinoa, or gluten-free bread.

Refried Beans

This recipe is for my good pal Nancy, who asked me if I could create a refried bean recipe that was actually good. I think these are great. Here you go! If you want, you can shortcut this with 3 cans of pintos or black beans, and of course, omit the water.

1 onion, peeled and halved

3 cups dry pinto beans, rinsed

½ fresh jalapeno pepper, seeded and chopped, optional

2 tablespoons minced garlic

4 teaspoons salt

2 teaspoons black pepper

¼ teaspoon ground cumin

9 cups water

Vegan cheddar and sour cream, optional

Place the onion, rinsed beans, jalapeno if using, garlic, salt, pepper, and cumin into a crock pot. Pour in the water and stir to combine. Cook on High for 8 hours, adding more water as needed. Once the beans are cooked, strain them, and reserve the liquid. Mash the beans with a potato masher, adding the reserved water as needed to attain desired consistency.

Black Bean and Cheese Burritos

If you want, you can eliminate the wrappers and just eat the filling with gluten-free pita chips, corn chips, or as a side dish. However, I tend to use my Chapatis instead of store bought wrappers, which I like a whole lot better.

1 green pepper, chopped

1 medium onion, chopped

1 garlic clove, minced

1 tablespoon olive oil

1 can of black beans, rinsed and drained

1 (14.5 ounce) can diced tomatoes, drained

1 tablespoon chili powder

1 teaspoon ground cumin

8 (6 inch) gluten –free flour tortillas, warmed, or chapatis

1 cup salsa

1 cup vegan cheddar, shredded

Sauté onions, peppers, and garlic in a little bit of oil, 3-5 minutes, or until the onions begin to brown. Stir in black beans and all spices, and simmer 10 minutes on low-medium heat. Add diced tomatoes and continue to cook until tomatoes are hot. Just before serving, stir in cheddar cheese and salsa.

Preheat oven to 350°F. Warm wrappers in the microwave just long enough to help them fold. Fill the 8 wrappers with the bean mix, adding optional cheese, salsa, and/or sour cream on top before baking. Cover pan with aluminum, and bake 15 minutes to help melt the cheese.

Black Bean Burgers

There are many variations for bean burgers, but this one works best for me. When I crave my old way of eating, I top with pickles, mustard, ketchup, fried onions, and a sprinkle of vegan cheddar, with a baked potato or my mac and cheese on the side. Use can also use kidney beans instead of black beans.

1 can of black beans, drained and rinsed

½ green bell pepper, diced small

½ of a medium onion, diced small

1 clove of garlic, minced

1 portion of egg replacer, prepared according to package instructions

1 tablespoon chili powder

1 tablespoon cumin

1 teaspoon hot sauce, optional

½ cup gluten-free bread crumbs, seasoned if desired with a pinch of oregano, salt, pepper, and paprika to taste

Preheat oven to 375°F and lightly oil a baking sheet. In a medium bowl, mash black beans with a fork or potato masher. Add diced vegetables and spices to beans. Stir in the egg replacer and mix in bread crumbs until the mixture is sticky and holds together. Divide mixture into four patties. If grilling, place patties on foil, and grill about 8 minutes on each side. If baking, place patties on baking sheet, and bake about 10 minutes on each side.

Tempeh Cacciatore

Tempeh is a fermented soybean product that originated in Indonesia. It is denser than tofu and is not water packed, so no draining is required. You can buy it plain or seasoned. I like Tofurky's varieties, which are gluten-free. Make sure you get an unflavored, gluten-free tempeh for this recipe. When in doubt, feel free to substitute with tofu or portabellas instead.

1 package gluten-free plain tempeh
4 tablespoons canola oil
1 teaspoon basil
1 teaspoon oregano
1 teaspoon of agave nectar
½ cup rice flour
1 cup chopped onions
1 (28ounce) can of tomato puree
1 clove of garlic, minced
salt, pepper, and other spices, to taste

Heat tempeh in a skillet for 5 minutes. Remove from heat and allow to cool. Mix together the flour, salt and pepper to make seasoned flour.

Preheat oven to 350°F. Dip each piece of tempeh in a shallow bowl of water, then in flour mixture until all pieces are coated.

Bake tempeh on a greased cookie sheet for 6 minutes, flip pieces, and bake another 6 minutes, or until it begins to brown.

Sauté onions and garlic in a large skillet in a little bit of oil, 3-5 minutes, until the onions begin to brown. In a large bowl, combine remaining ingredients and add to onions and garlic. Add tempeh slices to skillet. Cover and reduce heat, simmering for 30 minutes. Serve with your favorite gluten-free bread, pasta, rice, or potatoes.

Cherie's Awesome Soupy Beans

I am blessed with a large circle of loyal friends, and this recipe comes from one of my best buddies. This Indian dish typically calls for Ghee, which is off-limits for vegans, so she suggests you use oil as mentioned below. I use coconut oil and I think it's wonderful, but you can use any oil or vegan butter you wish. I'm sure you will love it as much as I do. This is quick, easy, and a versatile meal that can be served as a side dish or main meal, or, if you add more water, even as a soup.

2 cans of your favorite beans, any variety (or you can boil your own)
3 tablespoons of coconut or other oil
1 medium onion, chopped
4 cloves garlic, minced
½" to 1" piece of ginger root, chopped into tiny pieces
1 large or 2 medium tomatoes, diced
salt and pepper to taste
2 tablespoons of cilantro, fresh preferred

Heat oil in skillet, and add onion, garlic, and ginger. Sauté until the onions brown. Add the tomatoes, beans, and enough water to almost cover them. Simmer 20-30 minutes until tomatoes are soft and the mixture has thickened. You can add additonal water and make this into more of a soup, or allow more water to evaporate and serve as a bean dish. Add cilantro on top just before serving. Enjoy with brown rice, gluten-free tortillas, or other gluten-free item.

Bean Croquettes

I had these years ago before I was ever vegetarian or gluten-free, so when I first had to give up gluten, this was a comfort food. Personally, I like to serve these as the main course, with a side of broccoli and jasmine rice.

1 cup garbanzo bean flour
¾ cup hot water
juice of ½ lemon
2 teaspoons ground cumin
1 ½ teaspoons salt
15-oz can chickpeas (garbanzos), rinsed and drained well
4 scallions, chopped, green and white parts
½ red bell pepper, finely chopped
1 garlic clove, minced
1or more tablespoons of oil, for frying
non-stick cooking spray

In a large bowl, add flour, water, lemon juice, cumin, and salt. Stir until well combined. Add in chickpeas, scallions, and garlic. Stir well.

Coat a large skillet with non-stick spray. With your hands, form the croquette mixture into 8 egg shaped patties, about ½" thick. Place 4 patties in the pan, and cook 4-5 minutes, until the bottoms begin to brown. Add the frying oil, if desired, or use additional non-stick spray to keep the fat count low. With a spatula, flip patties, and cook 4-5 minutes on the other side, until that side begins to brown. Repeat with the remaining 4 patties. Serve alone, with rice, or other sides.

Italian Tofu

When compiling recipes for this cookbook, I almost forgot that tofu was in fact, a soybean product, and a couple of recipes rightfully belonged in this category. Of all my tofu creations, of which I have many, this one stood out. Blame the Italian in me, but I wanted to share something more than the usual stir fry.

½ cup gluten-free bread crumbs, seasoned with Italian herbs to taste

½ cup vegan parmesan cheese

salt and black pepper to taste

1 package firm tofu, drained and pressed of excess liquid

2 tablespoons olive oil

1 (8 ounce) can tomato sauce

½ teaspoon dried basil

1 clove garlic, minced

4 ounces shredded vegan mozzarella cheese

In a small bowl, combine bread crumbs, 2 tablespoons Parmesan cheese, salt, and black pepper. Slice tofu into ¼ inch thick slices, and place in bowl of cold water. One at a time, press tofu slices into crumb mixture, turning to coat all sides.

Heat oil in a medium skillet over medium heat. Use non-stick spray to reduce the amount of cooking oil needed, if desired. Cook until crisp on one side. Drizzle with a bit more olive oil, or recoat the pan, turn, and brown on the other side.

Preheat oven to 400° F. Combine tomato sauce, basil, garlic, and any other desired spices. Place a thin layer of sauce in an 8 inch square baking pan. Arrange tofu slices in the pan. Spoon remaining sauce over tofu. Top with vegan mozzarella and remaining parmesan. Bake for 20 minutes. Serve as a meal or as a tasty sandwich on your favorite gluten-free bread.

Barbeque Tofu Cubes

My answer to beef tips. Use in salads, in casseroles, stir fries, and just about any recipe that needs a sweet and spicy protein boost.

1 pound package of extra firm tofu, pressed and drained

¼ cup wheat-free tamari

2 tablespoons maple syrup

2 tablespoons ketchup

1 tablespoon vinegar

1 dash hot sauce (or more to taste), optional

1 teaspoon of agave nectar nectar

¼ teaspoon garlic powder

¼ teaspoon ground black pepper

Slice tofu into 1/2-inch slices, and gently press excess water out of tofu. Cut sliced tofu into 1/2-inch cubes. Stir together the tamari, maple syrup, ketchup, vinegar, and hot sauce if using. Add garlic powder and black pepper. Gently stir tofu cubes into sauce. Cover, and marinate at least one hour.

Preheat oven to 375°F. Lightly spray a non-stick baking sheet with oil. Place the tofu on a baking sheet in a single layer. Bake for 15 minutes, flip over, and bake for another 15 minutes until golden brown.

Grains

So much more than bread, whole grains provide a filling, inexpensive, and versatile meal that makes a lot and reheats well for leftovers.

When it comes to rice, brown unpolished rices are best for their fiber and vitamins, but you can definitely experiment with basmati, jasmine, and other varieties.

Corn Casserole

My good friend, Rondeana, is an awesome cook because she can make the simplest ingredients into easy, tasty recipes. Before I had to be gluten-free vegan, she came to my house and made this simple but hearty meal for me. It was one of the first I adapted to my new dietary needs, and one of the easiest. You can modify these basics to have variety. One of my favorites was Cammie's idea to add Newman's Peach Salsa on top jus before serving. Somehow, the sweet with the cheesy, creamy flavors is amazing! This recipe easily doubles or triples.

(1) 15 oz can kernel corn, include liquid
(1) 15 oz can creamed corn, undrained (this is dairy-free)
1 cup gluten-free elbow macaroni
½ cup melted vegan butter
½ cup vegan cheddar cheese

Preheat oven to 350°F. Grease a into a shallow 1 ½ quart casserole dish. Pour kernel corn (undrained), macaroni, margarine, and 1/4 cup of cheese into the dish and stir. Pour creamed corn slowly over the top of the mixture. Bake for 35 minutes. Sprinkle the remaining ¼ cup of cheese across the top and cook for an additional 5-10 minutes, or until top is slightly browned and macaroni is tender.

Mung Beans and Rice

This is a modernization of a recipe offered by my friend, Dave. Chances are he would not even recognize this as his original had I not asked to use it, but he did say everyone modifies it to suit their tastes. This is my favorite way to make this dish, but you can substitute other vegetables and spices for variety. What I like about it so much is that for convenience you can used canned and frozen ingredients, or use fresh produce when your garden is in season.

6 cups water or vegetable stock
1 cup jasmine rice
1 cup mung beans
1 small can of tomato sauce
1 large can of diced tomatoes including liquid, **or** 3 fresh tomatoes, diced
2 cups frozen green beans
1 can of diced potatoes, rinsed and drained
(1) 15 ounce can of kernel corn, rinsed and drained, **or** 2 cups frozen
(1) 15 ounce can of peas and carrots, rinsed and drained, **or** 2 cups frozen
1 teaspoon each oregano, minced garlic, onion powder, and paprika
2 teaspoons curry powder
a pinch of red pepper flakes, or something to add a hot and spicy "kick", optional
1 cup of vegan cheddar cheese, optional
fresh mung bean sprouts, optional

Place all ingredients, except for cheese and sprouts, in a large stockpot. Bring to a boil, then reduce heat and cover, stirring occasionally until the rice is done and the stock is absorbed, usually about 35-45 minutes. You may need to add more water or stock, so check throughout cooking time.

Once done, stir in the cheese and/or sprouts if using, and serve immediately. This recipe stores well and makes great leftovers for lunch.

Potato and Tofu Curry

Tofu and potatoes are favorites of mine, especially with this combination of spices. You can make this hot or mild. I prefer it on the spicy side, especially in the winter.

4 potatoes, peeled and cubed

2 tablespoons coconut oil

1 yellow onion, diced

2 cloves garlic, minced

2 teaspoons ground cumin

¼ teaspoon cayenne pepper, optional

4 teaspoons curry powder

1 (1 inch) piece fresh ginger root, peeled and minced

2 teaspoons salt

1 (14.5 ounce) can diced tomatoes, including liquid

1 (15 ounce) can garbanzo beans (chickpeas), rinsed and drained

1 (15 ounce) can peas, drained

1 (14 ounce) can regular or lite coconut milk

Place potatoes into a large pot and cover with water. Bring to a boil over high heat, then reduce heat and simmer until just tender, about 15 minutes. Drain. Meanwhile, heat the oil in a large skillet over medium heat. Stir in the onion and garlic; cook and stir until the onion has softened and turned translucent, about 5 minutes. Season with cumin, cayenne pepper, curry powder, ginger, and salt; cook for 2 minutes more. Add the tomatoes, garbanzo beans, peas, and potatoes. Pour in the coconut milk, and bring to a simmer. Simmer 5 to 10 minutes before serving.

Potatoes Au Gratin

This is another one of those recipes that simply did not go so well for me until I found Daiya cheddar. Hopefully, you can find it as well, but there are certainly other vegan cheeses that you could use.

4 russet potatoes, sliced into ¼ inch slices

1 onion, sliced into rings

salt and pepper to taste

3 tablespoons vegan butter

3 tablespoons all-purpose gluten-free flour

½ teaspoon salt

2 cups plain milk product

1 ½ cups shredded vegan cheddar cheese

Preheat oven to 400°F. Grease a 1 quart casserole dish. Layer ½ of the potatoes into bottom of the prepared casserole dish. Top with the onion slices, and add the remaining potatoes. Season with salt and pepper.

In a medium saucepan, melt butter over medium heat. Mix in the flour and salt, and stir constantly for one minute. Stir in the milk. Cook until mixture has thickened, then stir in cheese all at once, stirring until melted. Pour cheese over the potatoes, and cover the dish with aluminum foil. Bake 1 ½ hours.

Sweet Potato Casserole

This is a good replacement for the typical candied yams served at Thanksgiving.

4 ½ cups cooked and mashed sweet potatoes

½ cup vegan butter, melted

1/3 cup milk product

¾ cup maple syrup, regular or sugar-free

½ teaspoon vanilla extract

Egg replacer for 2 eggs, prepared according to package instructions

1 cup granulated sugar product

1 teaspoon molasses

½ cup gluten-free all-purpose flour

1/3 cup butter

1 cup chopped pecans

Preheat oven to 350°F. Grease a 9x13 inch baking dish.

In a large bowl, mix together mashed sweet potatoes, butter, milk, syrup, vanilla extract, and prepared egg replacer. Spread sweet potato mixture into the prepared baking dish. In a small bowl, mix together the granulated sweetener and flour. Cut in 1/3 cup butter until mixture is crumbly, then stir in pecans. Sprinkle pecan mixture over the sweet potatoes.

Bake for 25 minutes in the preheated oven, or until golden brown.

Corn and Spinach Enchiladas

You can make up a lot of these and freeze them for lunches, or just use the filling and serve with chips, salsa, and rice instead of as enchiladas.

1 tablespoon vegan butter

½ cup sliced green onions

1 clove of garlic, minced

1 (10 ounce) package frozen chopped spinach, thawed and pressed dry

½ cup vegan sour cream

1 cup shredded vegan cheddar cheese

10 (6 inch) corn tortillas

1 (19 ounce) can enchilada sauce

1 cup corn kernels, rinsed and drained

Preheat the oven to 375°F. Melt butter in a saucepan over medium heat. Add garlic and onion; cook for a few minutes until fragrant, but not brown. Stir in spinach, and cook for about 5 more minutes. Remove from the heat, and mix in sour cream, and ½ of the cheese.

In a skillet over medium heat, warm tortillas one at a time until flexible, about 15 seconds. Spoon about ¼ cup of the spinach mixture onto the center of each tortilla. Roll up, and place seam side down in a 9x13 inch baking dish. Pour enchilada sauce over the top, and sprinkle with the remaining cheese.

Bake for 15 to 20 minutes, until sauce is bubbling and cheese is lightly browned at the edges.

Risotto with Mushrooms and Asparagus

Risotto is not hard but can take some patience to make. I often use green beans instead of asparagus when they are in season.

6 ½ cups vegetable stock, divided

3 tablespoons olive oil, divided

1 pound portobella mushrooms, thinly sliced

1 pound white mushrooms, thinly sliced

2 shallots, diced

1½ cups Arborio rice

4 tablespoons vegan butter

¼ cup vegan Parmesan cheese

½ pound Asparagus tips

salt and pepper, to taste

In a saucepan, warm the broth over low heat. Warm 2 tablespoons oil in a large saucepan over medium-high heat. Stir in the mushrooms, and cook until soft, about 3 minutes. Remove mushrooms and their liquid, and set aside.

Add 1 tablespoon oil to skillet. Add rice, stirring to coat with oil, about 2 minutes. When the rice has taken on a pale, golden color, pour in ½ cup vegetable stock, stirring constantly until it is fully absorbed. Add ½ cup more broth to the rice, and stir until the broth is absorbed. Continue adding broth ½ cup at a time, stirring continuously, until the liquid is absorbed and the rice is al dente, about 15 to 20 minutes. Remove from heat, and stir in mushrooms with their liquid, butter, and parmesan. Season with salt and pepper to taste.

Quinoa Casserole

My good friend JoAn originally introduced me to Quinoa a few years ago when
I first had to avoid gluten, and I have been using it as a grain staple ever since.
This is equally good served hot or cold.

1/3 cup quinoa

1 cup water

1 pinch salt

1 tablespoon olive oil

1 teaspoon minced garlic

1 small sweet onion, chopped

1 cup mushrooms, sliced

salt and pepper to taste

Stir the quinoa in a saucepan over medium about 3 minutes. Pour in the water, and
add pinch of salt and pepper, if desired. Bring to a boil, then reduce heat to medium-
low, cover, and simmer until the quinoa is tender, about 20 minutes.

Meanwhile, heat the oil in a large skillet over medium heat. Stir in the garlic and
onion, and cook until the onion has softened, about 5 minutes. Add the mushrooms
and season to taste with salt and pepper. Cover the skillet, reduce heat to medium-
low, and cook about 10 minutes, stirring occasionally. Pour a splash of water into the
skillet if needed to keep the vegetables from burning. Spoon the vegetable mixture
over a bed of quinoa.

Quinoa Burgers

Of all of my veggie burgers, this is my favorite recipe. You can also bake these or grill outdoors on top of a sheet of aluminum foil.

1 ½ cups cooked quinoa

2/3 cup hummus

2 tablespoons tomato paste

2 tablespoons ground flaxseed meal

1 tablespoon tamari

1 teaspoon dried basil leaf

½ teaspoon paprika

½ teaspoon garlic powder

2 tablespoons garbanzo flour

Salt and pepper to taste

Blend all ingredients in a bowl or food processor until mashed. Divide burger mix into 8 equal portions and form into 3 inch patties. Fry in a little oil or use non-stick spray to coat a large skillet. Cook on medium heat, 5-8 minutes on each side, until browned and firm.

Serve on gluten-free buns and top with vegan cheese, ketchup, mustard, etc.

Spanish Rice Bake

There are many ways to make Spanish rice. This is my favorite way.

1 (15 ounce) can red beans, rinsed and drained

½ cup finely chopped onion

¼ cup chopped green bell pepper

1 (14.5 ounce) can canned tomatoes

1 cup water

¾ cup uncooked brown rice

½ cup chili sauce

1 teaspoon oregano

1 teaspoon agave nectar

½ teaspoon tamari

salt and pepper to taste

½ cup shredded vegan cheddar cheese

Combine all ingredients except the cheese. Simmer for about 45 minutes, stirring occasionally. Preheat oven to 375°F. Transport to a 2-quart casserole dish. Press firmly into dish and sprinkle with the cheese.

Bake for 10 to 15 minutes, or until cheese is melted.

Buckwheat with Leeks

Buckwheat is really a gluten-free grain that seems to be limited to pancakes but can be used instead of rice in almost any recipe. Here is my favorite way to prepare it.

1 cup whole buckwheat kasha
Egg replacer for 1 one egg, prepared according to instructions
2 cups vegetable stock
1 large leek, white portion only, cleaned and thinly sliced
1 cup sliced mushrooms
1 cup of frozen green peas
1 teaspoon of tamari
salt and pepper to taste

Prepare egg replacer. Combine with kasha. Heat a saucepan to low and add broth, tamari, salt and pepper. Stir well. Cover and let simmer for 20-25 minutes or until all liquid is absorbed.

Sauté leeks and mushrooms for about 5 minutes. Add frozen peas and cook until peas are defrosted. Remove kasha from heat. Stir in leeks and mushrooms.

Millet and Cabbage

My Facebook friends have read my countless messages of my love of cabbage.
Millet is a small gluten-free grain that is almost corn like in taste. It works really
well in this recipe, and any that would require the grain to almost take a "back seat"
such as stuffed peppers.

½ head of cabbage, chopped
4 stalks of boy choy, including leaves
1 small onion, chopped
1 cup of millet
2 teaspoons of wheat-free tamari
2 teaspoons, or more to taste, of gluten-free hoisin sauce
a pinch of red pepper flakes, optional

Prepare millet according to package instructions. Spray pan with non-stick spray.
Quickly Sauté all ingredients, including the millet, for about 5 minutes, or until
they achieve the desired level of softness. (I like mine a bit raw and crunchy).

Vegetables

I am a self-declared vegeholic and could easily never have a piece of meat or cup of rice again as long as I can have all the cooked vegetables I crave. Serve these as main courses or side dishes.

Biryani

Biryani is an Indian dish of select vegetables, spices, and meat/protein of choice. It is Persian for "fried" or "roasted", and is popular throughout south Asia. I reduced the overall fat, salt, and of course "veganized" it. It's a bit of work, and the ingredient list is a bit large, but it makes a lot and is well worth it. I like to have this with Naan.

2 tablespoons coconut or other oil

4 small potatoes, peeled and halved

2 large onions, finely chopped

2 cloves garlic, minced

1 tablespoon minced fresh ginger

½ teaspoon black pepper

½ teaspoon ground turmeric

1 teaspoon ground cumin

1 teaspoon salt

2 medium tomatoes, peeled and chopped

2 tablespoons plain vegan yogurt

1 large onion, diced

3 whole cloves

1 pound basmati or jasmine rice

4 cups vegetable stock

In a large skillet, fry potatoes in 2 tablespoons of coconut oil until brown. Add remaining 2 tablespoons of oil to the skillet and fry the onion, garlic, and ginger until onion is soft and golden. Add pepper, turmeric, cumin, salt, and tomatoes. Fry, stirring constantly, for 5 minutes. Add yogurt and cardamom. Cover and cook over low heat, stirring occasionally until the tomatoes turn to a pulp and the gravy is thickened.

In a large skillet, heat coconut oil and fry the cloves, ginger and rice. Stir continuously until the rice is coated with the spices. Add the stock and cover, reducing heat. Simmer 20 minutes, or until the stock is mostly absorbed and rice is done. Do not stir too frequently, but do check the stock level. You may need to add more water or stock. When the rice is done, combine the vegetable mixture to the same pot as the rice. Simmer on low heat an additional 20 minutes.

Stuffed Peppers

You can use buckwheat or millet in this recipe with equally yummy results.

2 cups quinoa

4 cups vegetable broth

1 tablespoon oil

2 scallions, both white and green parts, diced

¼ teaspoon salt

1 can (28 ounces) Italian style diced tomatoes

8 green bell peppers

2 cups of spinach or other leafy green

1 jar of your favorite tomato sauce

Cut tops off of peppers and remove seeds and membranes. Place them on a plate and microwave for 3 minutes to soften. Cook the quinoa in broth until soft and broth is absorbed, about 15-20 minutes. Heat oil in a skillet over medium heat and cook the onions for 2-3 minutes. Add the salt. Add the spinach/greens and quickly heat until wilted. Remove from heat. Add the quinoa and tomatoes and mix until combined. Stuff the peppers and place into a baking dish. Cover with aluminum or oven safe lid, and bake at 350°F for 30 minutes. While the peppers are cooking, heat your tomato sauce over low heat. Pour over peppers at time of serving.

Chow Mein

This simple meal is still one of my favorites. Serve with rice or noodles.

¼ cup vegan margarine

½ cup chopped mushrooms

2 cups chopped celery

2 onions, chopped

¼ teaspoon garlic powder

2 ½ cups veggie broth

2 teaspoons wheat free tamari

2 tablespoons cornstarch

1/3 cup cold water

1 pound drained and cubed tofu

In a wok or skillet, melt margarine over medium heat. Add mushrooms, celery, onions and garlic powder; cook until the onions have wilted. Add broth. Continue cooking until celery is cooked but still crisp. Stir in the tamari. Mix cornstarch and water together in a small bowl. Slowly stir into vegetables. Sauce should start to thicken a little. Mix in tofu, and heat through.

Vegetable Pot Pie

This took me quite some time to perfect, so do not get too hard on yourself if you have difficulty with the crust. It will taste just as good even if it gets crumbly, so you can sprinkle it on top, like dumplings, if you have trouble rolling them out and putting them in place.

Crust

2½ cups Gluten-Free All-Purpose Flour
2 teaspoons baking powder
1 teaspoon salt
1 cup vegan butter, chilled
1 cup vegan sour cream

Whisk together the first 3 ingredients in large bowl. Cut butter into chunks and cut them into the flour mixture with a fork or pastry cutter until flour turns into a coarse meal. Add in the sour cream and stir until dough forms.

Divide dough into two equal portions, and form into rounds. Place dough in the refrigerator for at least 30 minutes before using. After waiting, Roll out one and place it in a pie plate to be the bottom crust. Roll out the other and cut it into thin strips to make a lattice to top the pie or use as a full covering top crust (my preferred choice.)

Filling

3 tablespoons vegan butter
2½ cups chopped onions
16 ounce package of mushrooms, any variety, sliced
1 potato, diced
1 carrot, diced
½ cup frozen peas
2 stalks of celery, diced
1 (8-ounce) package vegan cream cheese

Melt butter in a large skillet over medium heat. Add onions and sauté until soft, about 3-5 minutes. Add mushrooms and portabellas, and cook until mushrooms are tender. Gently stir in cream cheese and remove from heat.

Preheat oven to 400°F. Spoon filling into uncooked pie crust and top with the second crust. Crimp edges of dough together. Cut a few slits in the top for proper venting. Bake 45 minutes or until crust is crispy and golden brown.

General Tso's Broccoli

Add optional tofu and other vegetables if desired, but I am such a broccoli freak, I eat it alone, with some leftover rice or noodles.

1 ½ cups granulated sugar product *or* ¾ cup agave nectar

¼ cup cider vinegar

¼ cup rice vinegar

2 ½ tablespoons tamari

2 teaspoons minced garlic

2 tablespoons vegetable oil

¼ cup ketchup, Organic preferred

12 dried whole red chilies, or to taste

2 tablespoons minced fresh ginger, or to taste

Heat the frying oil in a deep skillet. Combine the sweetener, vinegar, rice vinegar, tamari, ketchup, and garlic in a small saucepan. Bring to a boil over medium-high heat. Stir constantly until the sweetener has dissolved and the sauce thickens to the consistency of light pancake syrup, about 3 minutes. Remove from the heat and keep warm.

Bring 3 cups of water to a boil in a large pot. Drop broccoli florets into water and let cook for 1 minute, until it turns bright green. Remove and drain. Run cold water over broccoli to keep crisp.

Heat 2 tablespoons vegetable oil in a wok or large skillet over medium-high heat. Stir in the dried chiles and ginger; cook and stir until the ginger begins to brown, about 30 seconds. Remove the chiles and ginger from the wok and stir them into the sauce. Place the broccoli into the wok and cook until very crispy. Add sauce just before serving.

Spaghetti Squash Primavera

Until I found gluten-free pasta, I lived on spaghetti squash. It's always been a favorite of mine. If you are unfamiliar, it's an oblong round yellow squash, usually found with the acorn and butternut squashes. You scoop out seeds and when it's done, its stringy like angel hair pasta.

1 spaghetti squash, halved lengthwise and seeded

2 tablespoons oil

1 onion, chopped

1 clove garlic, minced

1 ½ cups chopped tomatoes

¾ cup vegan mozzarella cheese

3 tablespoons sliced black olives

2 tablespoons chopped fresh basil

Preheat oven to 350°F. Lightly grease a baking sheet.

Cut squash in half and remove all seeds. Place cut sides down on the prepared baking sheet, and bake 30 minutes or until a sharp knife can be inserted with only a little resistance. Remove squash from oven, and set aside to cool enough to be easily handled.

Meanwhile, heat oil in a skillet over medium heat. Sauté onion in oil until tender. Add garlic, and sauté for 2 to 3 minutes. Stir in the tomatoes, and cook only until tomatoes are warm.

Use a large spoon to scoop the stringy pulp from the squash, and place in a medium bowl. Toss with the sautéed vegetables, feta cheese, olives, and basil. Serve warm.

Cabbage Obsession

My friends have heard about my cabbage obsession on Facebook, so I had to share that recipe here. It's fairly simple and easily modified by different sauces and greens added. I usually like to have this with a baked potato, but its equally good with rice or noodles.

1 (15 ounce) can vegetable broth

1 small head of cabbage, cored and coarsely chopped

6 stalks of bok choy, including leaves, chopped

6 stalks of Napa cabbage, including leaves, chopped

2 cups dark leafy greens of choice (I usually use spinach)

½ teaspoon **each** of curry powder, ginger powder, and oregano

2 teaspoons of cornstarch or other starch

2 teaspoons of gluten-free hoisin sauce

Bring the broth to a boil in a large skillet. Reduce heat to low and add the cabbages, curry powder, ginger, and oregano. Cover and cook over medium heat for about 10 minutes, stirring frequently, or until cabbage is soft. Add greens and simmer just until wilted.

Dilute starch in a small amount of water, and add to vegetables to slightly thicken. Turn heat off. Add hoisin sauce and serve alone or with rice or noodles.

Greek Style Green Beans

There is a Greek restaurant in my town that makes something similar. I duplicated what I liked and eliminated what I did not.

6 cups of vegetable broth

1 (28 ounce) can tomato sauce

2 (14.5 ounce) cans green beans, drained and rinsed

1 large onion, chopped

2 cans (14.5 ounce) whole peeled potatoes

1 tablespoon seasoned salt

1 teaspoon black pepper

1 tablespoon garlic powder

Bring to a boil, then cover and simmer over low heat until meat falls off the bones, about 2 hours. Remove the bones and skin; return the meat to the pot. Discard bones and skin. Add the green beans to the Dutch oven and simmer for 20 minutes, then add the potatoes. Simmer for 10 to 15 minutes more, or until they can be easily pierced with a fork.

Cauliflower Casserole

I think cauliflower is an underrated vegetable, but its mild flavor lends it to really absorb the flavors of other foods prepared with it. Here, it gets to be the featured vegetable, but is so creamy, you might not even realize you are eating it.

1 large head cauliflower

½ cup seasoned gluten- free bread crumbs

2 tablespoons vegan Parmesan cheese

¼ cup vegan margarine, melted

¼ teaspoon salt

½ teaspoon **each** oregano, basil, and parsley

1 cup shredded vegan cheddar cheese

Preheat oven to 350°F. Bring 2 inches of water to a boil in a medium saucepan. Add cauliflower, cover, and cook for about 10 minutes. Drain, and place in a 2 quart casserole dish. In a small bowl mix together butter, cheese, bread crumbs, salt, and red pepper flakes. Sprinkle mixture over cauliflower, and top with cheese. Bake for 20 minutes, or until cheese is melted and bubbly.

Vegetable Burritos

I tend to use vegetables that are leftover from other recipes for these burritos, almost as one might make a stew, but when I make these "on purpose" this is the official recipe.

1 tablespoon olive oil

½ onion, chopped

1 cup diced zucchini

1 cup diced yellow squash

1 diced red pepper

½ cup broccoli florets, chopped small

½ cup cauliflower florets, chopped small

salt and pepper to taste

½ teaspoon chili powder

4 (7 inch) gluten-free tortillas

½ cup shredded vegan cheddar cheese

½ cup chopped tomato

Heat the olive oil in a skillet over medium-high heat; cook and stir the onion and pepper in the hot oil until fragrant, about 3 minutes. Next, add the broccoli, cauliflower, and the squashes in three batches, making sure the first has softened slightly before adding the next. Season with salt.

Heat the tortillas in the microwave until warm, about 10 seconds. Spoon the squash mixture into the center of the tortillas; top with the cheese and tomato. Roll into a burrito to serve.

Korma

Korma is an Indian dish that often calls for large amounts of cream, butter, and meat. Use lite coconut milk, or plain soymilk to keep the fat even lower.

1 ½ tablespoons vegetable oil

1 small onion, diced

1 teaspoon minced fresh ginger root

4 cloves garlic, minced

2 potatoes, cubed

4 carrots, cubed

3 tablespoons ground unsalted cashews

½ cup tomato sauce

2 teaspoons salt

1 ½ tablespoons curry powder

1 cup frozen green peas

½ green bell pepper, chopped

½ red bell pepper, chopped

1 cup lite coconut milk, or plain milk product

Heat the oil in a skillet over medium heat. Stir in the onion, and cook until tender. Mix in ginger and garlic, and continue cooking 1 minute. Mix potatoes, carrots, cashews, and tomato sauce. Season with salt and curry powder. Cook and stir 10 minutes, or until potatoes are tender. Stir peas, green bell pepper, red bell pepper, and coconut milk into the skillet. Reduce heat to low, cover, and simmer 10 minutes before serving.

Eggplant Rollatini

The first time I had this recipe, I was convinced it was the best food on the planet. When I look back now to how much fat, salt, and cheese was in it, well no wonder I loved it so much. However, those days of gorging are behind me, and so this trimmed down heart-healthy version works as a main course or appetizer. Serve with pasta or salad to keep calories under control.

1 eggplant, peeled and cut lengthwise into 1/4 inch slices

1 cup milk product

1 cup Italian seasoned gluten-free bread crumbs

2 tablespoons oil

(14 ounce) jar spaghetti sauce

3 cups vegan mozzarella cheese

Dip the eggplant slices in milk product, then coat with bread crumbs. Use non-stick spray with a bit of oil in a large skillet over medium-high heat. Fry the eggplant on each side until golden brown. Remove to a paper towel lined plate to drain.

Preheat the oven to 350°F. Sprinkle a thin layer of vegan cheese onto each slice of eggplant. Roll up tightly, and place seam side down in a 9x13 inch baking dish. Pour spaghetti sauce over the rolls, and top with more cheese.

Bake for 15 minutes until the cheese is melted and lightly browned.

Mexican Mushrooms and Cheese Bake

You could turn this into enchiladas for variety, or cook totally without the corn tortillas and add a can of drained and rinsed corn instead.

1 (15 ounce) can tomato sauce

1 (6 ounce) can tomato paste

1 teaspoon chili powder

1 (12 ounce) package corn tortillas

1 (8 ounce) package vegan Cheddar cheese, divided

1 onion, diced

1 (6 ounce) can sliced ripe olives

1 (6 ounce) can sliced mushrooms

Preheat oven to 350°F. In a medium bowl, combine tomato sauce, tomato paste and chili powder. Warm the tortillas in the microwave, then dip them in the tomato sauce mixture. Prepare in a large round casserole dish or baking pan. Place a layer of corn tortillas on the bottom, add the vegetables and cheese, then sauce, then another layer of tortillas until you are out of all ingredients or run out of room. Bake for 25 to 30 minutes, or until cheese is melted and bubbly.

Roasted Vegetables

Use whatever is available. This is a good way to cook up vegetables at the end of the week that were unused before your next shopping trip. Place on top of salads, make into sandwiches, etc.

2 zucchini, sliced into matchsticks

2 red bell peppers, seeded and diced

1 sweet potato, peeled and cubed

1 cup of mushrooms, sliced

1 red onion, quartered

1 tablespoon oregano

1 teaspoon minced garlic

¼ cup oil

2 tablespoons balsamic vinegar

salt and freshly ground black pepper

Preheat oven to 475°F. In a large bowl, combine the squash, red bell peppers, onion, mushrooms, and zucchini.

In a small bowl, stir together garlic, oregano, olive oil, vinegar, salt, and pepper. Toss with vegetables until they are coated. Spread evenly on a large roasting pan.

Roast for 35 to 40 minutes, stirring every 10 minutes, or until vegetables are cooked through and browned. Serve alone, or on top of potatoes, rice, or noodles.

Drinks

Sorry to get your hopes up- nothing alcoholic here! Instead, you will find healthy, yummy, creamy drinks that are dessert worthy and crowd pleasing.

Berry Lemonade

I think back to my childhood, when my mother innocently mixed up lemonade from a powder. It was way inferior to this recipe, high in sugar, and low in anything other than chemicals. Lemons are very antibiotic and detoxifying to the system, so I try to have them as often as possible.

1½ cups agave nectar

9 cups water

2 cups fresh lemon juice

2 (10 ounce) package frozen strawberries, partially thawed

In a large pitcher, mix together lemon juice, agave nectar and water. Add strawberries to a blender or food processor, and blend just until they are pulverized and juicy. Stir berries into lemonade. Chill before serving.

Cherry Limeade

Limes are just as good for you as lemons, and are a natural remedy for depression, especially in the winter months and for those who have SAD.

1 cup fresh squeezed lime juice

5 cups water

¾ cup agave nectar nectar

1 (10 ounce) jar maraschino cherries, drained and juice reserved

In a pitcher, combine lime juice, water, sugar and honey. Stir in reserved cherry juice. Stir until sugar is dissolved. Chill in refrigerator. Garnish with cherries and lime slices.

Cranberry Iced Tea

You can certainly use any juice you wish, as long as its 100% real.

1 gallon water

1 cup of agave nectar

15 green tea bags, regular or caffeine-free

1 cup cranberry juice, preferably unsweetened

Put water in large pot, and heat on high until boiling. Add agave nectar and stir until dissolved. Add teabags and let steep until desired strength is acquired. Stir in cranberry juice, and allow to cool.

Creamy Iced Coffee

I do not care for hot coffee too much, but its one of my favorite cold drinks.

4 cups fresh brewed coffee

1 teaspoon vanilla extract

½ cup agave nectar

¼ cup boiling water

3 cups crushed ice

½ cup vanilla milk product or Mimic Crème

Refrigerate coffee until cool, about 30 minutes. Stir vanilla extract and agave nectar in the boiling water until dissolved. Refrigerate until cool, about 30 minutes. Stir in cream and additional sweetener, to taste. Pour over ice.

Orange Creamcicle

I am normally not much of a juice drinker, but this is really good and reminds me of those ice cream bars.

2 cups fresh orange juice

2 cups vanilla milk product

2 scoops vanilla non-dairy ice cream

¾ cup agave nectar

1 teaspoon vanilla extract

12 ice cubes

Place all ingredients in a blender, and process until ice is slushy.

Cookies and Cream Milkshake

My guilty pleasure. I really can overdo it here, so I actually try to not have these ingredients on hand! I've given this to several others who had no idea it was dairy-free, so I think its safe to say if you're reading this, you will too. Change it out with different types of cookies and flavored non-dairy ice cream.

2 cups vanilla non-dairy ice cream

1 cup vanilla milk product

1 teaspoon vanilla extract

4 gluten-free vegan oreo-style cookies, broken

Place all ingredients in blender and process until smooth and thick.

Almond Milk

When I first realized how easy it was to make this, I couldn't stop making it! Now that the novelty is worn off, I make a batch every now and then and freeze the leftovers.

1 cup almonds

2 ½ cups Water

1 teaspoon of vanilla extract

½ cup rice syrup

Bring about 1 cup of water to a boil in your pot. Drop in your almonds. Let them boil for about 3 minutes and then pour everything through a strainer so that the water pours out and you're left with just the almonds. Pour the almonds out onto a plate and let them rest for a few minutes until they are cool enough to touch with your hands.

Place almonds and water into a blender of food processor in small batches. Blend until the nuts are chopped fine. Repeat until all almonds and water have been used.

Position a mesh strainer or other strainer lined with cheesecloth over a large bowl. Strain the nuts and water, keeping the water. Add vanilla and rice syrup. Stir and refrigerate.

Minty Hot Chocolate

This can also be served chilled, if desired. Another recipe I can drink too much of, so I see this as more of a dessert drink.

3 cups chocolate milk product

1/3 cup vegan chocolate chips

2 tablespoons agave nectar or rice syrup

¼ teaspoon peppermint extract

vegan whipped cream or whipped topping

Put milk into a microwave-safe container and heat for 2 minutes. Mix in chocolate, then return it to microwave and cook on High for 3 to 4 minutes, being careful not to let it boil. Whisk in sweetener and peppermint. Top with whipped topping if desired.

Spiced Cider

I first had spiced cider of this style at a women's empowerment group. I remember very little from the classes, but I do remember this recipe.

6 cups apple cider

¼ cup maple syrup

2 cinnamon sticks

6 whole cloves

1 inch piece of ginger

1 lemon peel, cut into strips

1 tablespoon dried dandelion root, optional

1 tablespoon dried burdock root, optional

Pour the apple cider and maple syrup into a large stainless steel saucepan. Place the cinnamon sticks, cloves, burdock, dandelion, and lemon peel in the center of a washed square of cheesecloth; fold up the sides of the cheesecloth to enclose the bundle, then tie it up with a length of kitchen string. Drop the spice bundle into the cider mixture.

Place the saucepan over moderate heat for 5 to 10 minutes, or until the cider is very hot but not boiling.

Remove the cider from the heat. Discard the spice bundle. Ladle the cider into big cups or mugs, adding a fresh cinnamon stick to each serving if desired.

Creamy Green Drink

For the record, I am NOT one of those vegans who adores juicing and raw foods. I admire those types, but try as I might, I typically hate green drinks. I was relieved to be allergic to wheatgrass because I hated it so much! This one however, was made totally by accident, and is so yummy, I do not even taste the kale. If you are one of those who loves green drinks, you might find this a tad sweet, but I assure you, it's good for you. Just omit the rice syrup or add more kale.

1 banana, thickly sliced, frozen

2 cups chopped kale

¼ cup vanilla milk product

1/3 cup orange juice

2 teaspoons rice syrup

1 teaspoon vanilla extract

Place the banana, kale, vanilla, and coconut oil into a blender, pour in the milk and orange juice. Cover, and puree until smooth. Add rice syrup and serve.

Breakfast Smoothie

This is my drink of choice when I am overheated, hungry, and yet have no desire to eat. Its also good for those who like juice fasting but find blood sugar swings get in the way of true fasting.

½ cup vanilla milk product

½ cup vanilla soy yogurt

½ frozen banana, peeled and chopped

2 tablespoons powdered vegan protein supplement

1 ½ tablespoons flax seed meal

1 teaspoon agave nectar

1 tablespoon almond or other nut butter of choice

½ cup frozen blueberries

In a blender, blend the milk, yogurt, banana, protein supplement, flax seed, honey, and blueberries until smooth.

Melon Cooler

This is a yummy, slushy drink for BBQ's and other fun summer events.

2 cups cubed seedless watermelon

2 cups honeydew melon

10 ice cubes

1/3 cup fresh lime juice

¼ cup agave nectar

Place watermelon and ice into a blender. Pour in lime juice and agave nectar. Blend until smooth.

Snacks

We conclude our book with quick to prepare snacks. Some are more dessert-like while others are good for everyday eating. Hopefully, these give you some great holiday gifting ideas as well.

Maple Roasted Walnuts

These are simple to make, and make the whole house smell great. I put them in jars and give them away as holiday gifts.

2 cup walnuts
4 tablespoons maple syrup
4 tablespoons granulated sweetener (I use stevia)
1 teaspoon of cinnamon

Preheat oven to 350F. Combine all ingredients in small bowl, and toss to coat. Spread pecans on a foil-covered baking sheet. Bake 20 to 30 minutes, stirring every 10 minutes, until sugar is caramelized. Set pan on wire rack, and let cool 10 minutes.

Cashew Brittle

I love cashew brittle, but not the corn syrup. I discovered that using real maple syrup, or sugar-free for those who cannot have sugar, works equally well and is way better for you. This makes a lot, so I suggest making goodie bags for friends.

2 cups granulated sugar product

1 cup maple syrup

½ cup water

1 cup vegan butter

3 cups cashews

1 teaspoon baking soda

Grease two cookie sheets and set out, for ease of preparation, all the ingredients in easy to reach containers, as this recipe doesn't allow for much time in between steps, though preparation is very easy to do.

In a large saucepan, combine granulated sweetener, maple syrup, and water. Cook over medium heat, stirring, until sugar product dissolves. Bring to a boil and blend in butter product. Begin to stir frequently when syrup reaches the thread stage, about 280°F. You can use either a candy thermometer for this, or do what I do which is drop a tiny amount in a glass of water. If it turns instantly into hardened candy threads, it's done.

Add cashews to candy mixture, and stir constantly. Allow mixture to get warm again, up to 300°F, or until the mixture passes the thread test again.

Remove from heat and quickly stir in baking soda. Mix well then pour onto the two buttered baking sheets. Carefully pick up sheets using pot holders and move the sheets around, helping the candy spread. Allow to set about 10 minutes, then loosen from the pans as soon as possible and turn over. Break hardened candy up and store in an airtight container.

S'mores

I thought I would have to give these up until I found Rice Mellow a gluten-free, vegan marshmallow-like fluff. Besides, since creating my gluten-free vegan graham recipe for my previous book, I've been searching far and wide for a safe marshmallow product. These are super easy to make and quick.

12 gluten-free vegan graham crackers
1 ½ cups Ricemellow Creme
¾ cup vegan chocolate chips

Spread a portion of fluff on 6 of the grahams until no more is left. Melt chips in a microwave safe container for 30 seconds, stirring as needed. Spread chocolate on the remaining 6 grahams, then sandwich together.

Crispy Treats

This is another recipe that would not be possible (for me) without Rice Mellow! This quick and easy recipe only has three ingredients. Feel free to add chocolate chips, nuts, dried fruit, or other optional stir-ins.

6 cups gluten-free crispy rice cereal
2 cups Rice Mellow or similar product available
1 tablespoon of vegan butter

Melt margarine in a large pot. Reduce temperature and add Rice Mellow. Stir in cereal. Use a greased spoon to help mix cereal until well coated. Press into a greased 9x13 pan. Allow to cool 15 minutes before serving.

Peanut Butter Candy Cups

I make these in mini muffin tins, but you certainly can increase them up to full size muffin tins or other candy molds of your choice.

2 cups of chunky peanut butter

1½ sticks vegan butter

2 ½ cups of granulated sugar product

2 ½ cups of gluten-free graham cracker crumbs

2 tablespoons of vanilla

1 bag of vegan chocolate chips

½ cup dried blueberries or other dried fruit, such as raisins, optional

Melt the peanut butter and the butter together. Remove peanut butter and butter mixture from heat. Add sugar, crumbs and vanilla. Press mixture into greased mini muffin or other size tin or mold of choice.

Melt the chocolate in a double boiler or microwave, stirring to make sure it does not burn. Add dried blueberries or other dried fruit,, if desired. Pour melted chocolate over the peanut butter mixture. Refrigerate for 10 minutes or more before removing from tins/molds.

Trail Mix

I find that traditional nuts can get soggy in a trail mix, which is why I used soy nuts and seeds. You can of course add any nuts you wish if slightly soft nuts will not bother you.

½ cup dried prunes

½ cup dried apricots

½ cup dried pineapple chunks

½ cup raisins

1 cup sunflower seeds

½ cup pumpkin seeds

1 cup of soy nuts

Pinch of salt, if desired

Combine all ingredients and store in an airtight container.

Party Mix

A great gift idea with easy clean up and minimum fuss.

3 cups gluten-free cereal
1 cup nuts
1 cup air popped (unbuttered) popcorn
1 cup gluten-free pretzels (such as Glutino)
2 tablespoons vegan butter
1 tablespoon tamari
½ teaspoon garlic powder
½ teaspoon onion powder
½ teaspoon salt product
1 teaspoon vegan parmesan

Microwave butter 30 seconds until melted. Stir in tamari, salt, onion, and garlic.
In a large bowl microwave safe container, combine all other ingredients. Pour
butter over mix. Microwave the mix 5 minutes, stirring every minute. Store in an
airtight container.

Candy Apples

Candy Apples remind me of trips to the Boardwalk at Seaside Heights.

8 medium sized apples (I prefer Macintosh)
8 wooden sticks
3 cups granulated sugar product
½ cup maple syrup
1 cup water
¼ teaspoon gluten-free red food coloring

Wash and dry the apples. Remove any stems or leaves and insert a wooden stick into the end of each apple. Set apples aside.

Heat sweetener, syrup, and water in a saucepan until sugar has dissolved. Boil until the syrup reaches 300°F on a candy thermometer, or until a little syrup dropped into cold water forms threads.

Remove from heat. Dip one apple completely into the candy and stir until apple is covered. Hold the apple above the saucepan to drain off excess. Place apple, with the stick facing up, on a well greased pan.

Repeat with remaining apples. If candy thickens or cools too much, simply reheat briefly before proceeding. Let cool completely before serving.

Cinnamon Pita Chips

My favorite crunchy snack. I really love cinnamon, so it's no wonder. I try not to make too many only because in time they lose their crunch, but you can double or triple the recipe.

3 large gluten-free pita pockets

3 tablespoons granulated sugar product

3 tablespoons melted vegan butter or coconut oil

2 teaspoons cinnamon

Preheat oven to 400°F. Line a cookie sheet with aluminum foil. Grease foil with non-stick spray or oil of choice.

Cut pita pockets into triangles and place on cookie sheet. Using a brush, coat each triangle with the melted butter.

Sprinkle sugar and cinnamon over triangles. Bake for 6-8 minutes, depending on thickness of pita bread. Pitas should be very crispy when done.

Coconut Chews

Every now and then, I get a really strong coconut craving, and this really hits the spot. This recipe can yield a lot candy, up to 60 pieces depending on the size of the balls you make. I suggest freezing or bringing the leftovers to your next gathering.

½ cup vegan butter

1 cup chopped dates

¾ cup granulated sugar product

Egg replacer for 2 eggs, prepared according to box instructions

1 cup chopped pecans

1 cup gluten-free crispy rice cereal

1 teaspoon vanilla extract

2 cups flaked coconut, unsweetened

In a saucepan, melt butter over low heat. Stir in the dates, sugar, and egg replacer. Cook and stir over low heat for 10 minutes. Remove from heat and stir in the pecans, cereal, and vanilla.

When cool enough to handle, shape into 1 inch balls, then roll in coconut. Place on greased baking sheets. Refrigerate for 1-2 hours or until firm. Store in an airtight container in the refrigerator.

Crunchy Roasted Chick Peas

So much lower in fat than nuts, but higher in protein. I actually like these as croutons in salads or a big handful when I have some dried fruit.

1 (15 ounce) can chickpeas, drained, rinsed, and allowed to dry
1 tablespoon olive oil
1 teaspoon curry powder
½ teaspoon garlic powder
½ teaspoon salt product, optional

Heat the oven to 400°F. Heat the oil in a small pan over low heat, then add the curry and garlic powders, and cook for 3 minutes.

Turn off the heat, add the chickpeas, and stir gently stir until they're well-coated.

Spread them out a foil-lined rimmed cookie sheet and bake for 50 minutes. You'll know they're done when they begin to get golden and crunchy.

Popcorn Balls

So much easier to make than I originally thought, and a great gift or treat idea.

½ cup popcorn kernels

3 tablespoons coconut oil

½ teaspoon salt product

½ cup maple syrup

½ cup rice syrup

Pop popcorn in an air popper. Mix maple and rice syrups in a small sauce pan, and bring to a boil. Lower heat to medium-low, and stir constantly for 5-6 minutes. Pour the hot syrups over the popcorn and mix thoroughly. Slightly moisten your hands with cold water, and form balls by firmly packing the mixture with your hands. Be sure to moisten your hands before making each ball. Place balls in a covered container or wrap in wax paper, then freeze until the syrup hardens.

Featured Products

Daiya Foods www.daiyafoods.com
Ener-g Egg Replacer www.ener-g.com
Bob's Gluten-free Flours www.bobsredmill.com
Now Foods www.nowfoods.com
Jules Gluten-free flour www.julesglutenfree.com
Barry Farms www.barryfarms.com
Earth Balance www.earthbalancenatural.com
Mimic Crème www.mimiccreme.com
Rice Mellow www.Suzannes-specialties.com
So Delicious non-dairy ice cream www.turtlemountain.com
San-J gluten-free Asian sauces www.san-j.com

About the Author

Dawn Grey, PhD, is a Certified Holistic Health Practitioner and owner of the Aruna Center of Lawrence, Kansas. After discovering her lifelong health issues were the results of dairy, egg, and wheat sensitivities in 2001, she changed her diet and the scope of her consultation business to help others identify and manage their own sensitivities. Now, nine years later, she is healthier, leaner, and happier than ever before.

Dawn is available for personal wellness coaching by special appointment. For more information about being a distance client of the Aruna Center, please contact Dawn at **reikirays@yahoo.com**

For additional holistic and metaphysical services, please visit her website at **www.arunacenter.com**

In addition to this book, Dawn is the author of ***New Dawn Kitchen: Gluten-Free, Vegan, and Easily Sugar-Free Desserts*** and ***Insight Tarot.***

For those interested in learning more about holistic and natural methods of health and healing, Dawn and her staff over accredited distance education courses at **www.reikiraysinstitute.com**

Visit **www.newdawnkitchen.com** for some pictures of featured recipes in this book, as well as her Facebook page, the Virtuous Vegan.

Made in the USA
Charleston, SC
04 August 2010